ᴏREST SYSTEM

D0387361

Superior

ᴘpewa   Chequamegon   Ottawa   Hiawatha

Nicolet   Huron

nnesota   Wisconsin   Manistee

Iowa   Michigan

Eastern Region   Ohio   Wayne

Missouri   Illinois   Indiana   Monongahela

Hoosier   West   George
Virginia   Washington

Shawnee   Daniel   Jefferson
Boone

Mark Twain   Kentucky   Virginia

Cherokee   Pisgah   Uwharrie
Nantahala

Ozark   Tennessee   North Carolina

Arkansas   Holly Springs   Croatan

St. Francis   William B.   Sumter
Bankhead   Chattahoochee   South Carolina

Ouachita   Oconee

addo   Mississippi   Alabama   Talladega   Francis Marion

Sabine   Tombigbee   Georgia

Kisatchie   Delta   Bienville   Tuskegee

ᴠy   Homochitto   Conecuh   Choctawhatchee
ᴄkett   Desoto   Apalachicola

Angelina   Osceola

m Houston   Louisiana   Ocala

Florida

Southern Region

Maine

Vermont   White Mountain

Green Mountain   New Hampshire

New York   Massachusetts

Finger Lakes   Rhode Island
Connecticut

Allegheny

Pennsylvania   New Jersey

Maryland   Delaware
Washington, D.C.

National Forests
National Grasslands

Caribbean
Puerto Rico

CLEARCUTTING:

A Crime Against Nature

CLEARCUTTING:
A Crime Against Nature

Edward C. Fritz

EAKIN PRESS

(All photographs by author unless other credit given.)

Table of Contents

Foreword

Citizen concern over disastrous clearcutting practices led to the passage of the National Forest Management Act of 1976. This was believed to be a conservation victory that would produce sounder forest management and greatly limited used of clearcutting as a practice on our national forests. Congress said that clearcutting is to be used only where it is the optimum method. In spite of this congressional direction and continuing citizen concern, more than ten years after NFMA, the Forest Service continues to use clearcutting as the dominant practice even for highly scenic areas and intends to continue high levels of clearcutting for the next fifty years. For example in 1984 the Forest Service cut 615,000 acres of forest land. In that year only 85,000 acres were selectively harvested.

Clearcutting is a very questionable practice on public lands. Unquestionably, clearcutting has large impacts on the other multiple uses and resources of the forest. A clearcut is the epitome of a single use excluding other uses for some time. Its impacts extend well beyond the area affected. Frequently clearcuts and the accompanying roads pollute streams and destroy valuable fisheries. Clearcuts are ugly. In mountainous terrain clearcuts ruin scenic beauty for miles. A most critical concern is the effect clearcutting may have on biological diversity. I personally consider the loss of biological diversity the most important problem facing the planet. In this country we have a major opportunity to protect biological diversity through our public lands, especially national forests. Unfortunately, Forest Service plans for the national forests will reduce their natural diversity. Large scale use of clearcutting will reduce diversity causing loss of valuable biological and genetic resources and leaving these timber stands vulnerable to future insect and disease attacks. Ironically, there are also sound economic arguments for maintaining diversity. Long term commitments to a "single product" is a risky business. Timber yield and profits can frequently be higher with uneven age management due to improved growth, higher quality products, and reduction in costs.

It is my opinion and I believe it was the intention of the Congress in passing the National Forest Management Act — that the use of clearcutting on the national forests should be limited to exceptional cases. Ten years is long enough to wait for the Forest Service to implement the will of the people. It is time for an all out campaign for ecologically sound forestry.

Clearcutting: A Crime Against Nature stimulates efforts for real reform. Ned Fritz accurately describes and graphically shows the abuses showered upon the national forests by its managers — the Forest Service. It is intended to arouse the public and our elected officials finally to action. The author has been a courageous advocate and an untiring student of forest management. This could be Mr. Fritz's finest contribution yet to conservation.

By Barry R. Flamm
Chief Forester
The Wilderness Society

Preface

From one end of this nation to the other, the Forest Service and other federal agencies are engaged in wholesale clearcutting.

The color plates show what a clearcut looks like for a while (photographs 1–16, clearcuts in sixteen National Forests, from East to West Coast.)

This most catastrophic harvesting method is wiping out native plants and animals. The Red-cockaded woodpecker has declined precipitously as clearcutting has fragmented its foraging habitat. In Texas, for example, that endangered species declined approximately 76% to 190 colonies in four national forests in only ten years — 1978–1987. Aggravating the jeopardy, the colony size shrank to an average of only 2.4 birds. A large number of colonies contain only the male. Regeneration is not taking place in those colonies.

It does not have to be like that.

After hearing all the evidence and argumentation that the Forest Service could muster, an impartial tribunal on October 20, 1988, banned clearcutting from 200,000 acres, a third of the available commercial timber in four national forests in East Texas.

U.S. District Judge Robert M. Parker exploded the Forest Service's well-cultivated myth that where forests are harvested, clearcutting is generally the best method.

The Judge held that selection management is better than clearcutting (even-age management), both economically and environmentally. It is more cost-effective and will produce as much timber, at least in the Southern pine belt where the Red-cockaded woodpecker survives.

Color plates 17–25 show how forests under selection management look every year, including years when logged (once every ten years or so).

In 1988, as in an early 1970 uprising, the major newspapers, magazines, and television networks, have presented both sides of the clearcutting controversy in capsule form.

In an academic way, several recent books about national forest practices have recognized the problems of clearcutting. Many researchers, mainly funded by the Forest Service or timber industry, have addressed specific sub-topics, such as water run-off from various types of site preparation.

Some foresters have defined the even-age and selection management systems, usually opining that each system has its place, depending on the conditions of stands. Independent foresters like Leon S. Minckler (*Woodland Ecology*, 1975), Charles H. Stoddard (*Essentials of Forestry Practices*, 1978), and Gordon Robinson (*The Forest and the Trees*, 1987), extolled selection management. Randal O'Toole (*Forest Service Reform*, 1988) brushes off clearcutting restraint as a "prescription" approach, which he says Congress will not pass. He is not an expert in getting Congress to pass legislation. Congress recently restrained clearcutting in the Ouachita National Forest in Oklahoma.

None of the authors has provided an in-depth critical examination of clearcutting versus selection management. Since clearcutting is by far the most widespread evil in our forests, the nation deserves such an examination.

I long considered writing this book in the journalistic tradition, presenting the pros and cons with an air of objectivity. But others have approached some of the clearcutting issues in that fashion without stirring up the mass conflagration that is necessary to effectuate reform. This book presents all the arguments, both ways. To those of us who have heard both sides, it has become crystal clear that there is no sound basis for continuing with pervasive clearcutting in our national forests. Therefore, I propose a course of action to restrain the practice, and to return our forests to the people.

Acknowledgments

First and last, thanks to Genie, who word processed the living daylights out of all my continuous drafting, and threw in some good suggestions, as well. Genie also assisted on all out-of-state forays, except the flight East.

Accolades for the volunteer photographers credited on the plates: Brad Moore, who participated in our 1987 forest storming flight through the East; my old friend, Charles H. Stoddard, Wisconsin forester, and Christopher Runk, Dallas conservationist; Glenn C. Smith, West Virginia wildlife photographer; Jess Alford, Jr., principal photographer of my second book, *Realms of Beauty*; George H. Russell, Forest Practices chair of the Sierra Club, Lone Star Chapter; James R. Jackson and Larry Shelton, my premier guides in Texas; James Norman, tireless Arkansan; Randall L. Kuipers in Michigan; and, from the West, Diane Kelsay, James R. Conner, David Parker, Trygve Steen, Patrick Carr; from Project Lighthawk, Michael M. Stewartt, and in Alaska, J. Warren. If you see no credit by a photograph, I took it.

Ole for Charles Jamieson, our trusted pilot on the Eastern tour, and to Project Lighthawk for encouraging pilots like Charlie.

Appreciation to Anne Weary, David Wilson and Billy Hallmon for their graphics.

Gratitude to those who hosted and guided us on our 1986 jaunt from Dallas to Denali: Robert Brothers (in absentia) and Mountain Man, of Williams, Oregon; Pete and Greta Sorenson of Eugene; Steve Kallick, Peter and Kate Isleib, and son, Ned, of Juneau; Craig Mapes, of Tenakee Springs, Alaska; David and Joey Knepp, in Anchorage; Tom Campion of Seattle; and James R. Jackson much of the way.

Hurrahs for our hosts and guides on the fabulous flight East: Will McDearman and Carrie Norquist, Mississippi; Frank Stewart, Jr., Alabama; Dr. Wilson Baker and Ira Bohn, Florida; Ken Combs, Georgia; John Doyal and Ron Tipton, Tennessee; Dr. Leon S. Minckler and Ernie Dickerman, Virginia; Gayle Fritz (my second daughter) and Rose McCullough, Washington, D.C.; Mary Wimmer, West Virginia; Andy Mahler and Linda Lee, Indiana; Mark Donham and Kristy Hanson, Illinois; John Karel, Missouri.

And thanks to our mentors on our California caravan, forester Gordon Robinson; Wisconsin wandering, forester Charles Stoddard; Arkansas aberrations, Mike and Andrea Crawford, Jerry Williams, and James Norman; Michigan mission, Randall L. Kuipers, forester; Vermont visit, the late, great Red Arnold; and Texas tours, Larry Shelton, James R. Jackson, George and Sue Russell, forester Bill Carroll, John Ward, Dan Northcut, Pat Paradies, and Mike Harrison.

Plaudits to those who helped to proof-read and to index: Martha Gene Beaty, Billie Woodard, Alison Blackhall, Jeannette Crawford, and Morine Kovich.

Those who have provided peer review on various segments include Randal O'Toole, Beth Johnson, George Russell, Mike Frome, and Walton Smith.

Dr. Michael Warnock, of Sam Houston State University, listed for us the plants that are most susceptible to clearcuts.

Forest Service personnel who were both informative and considerate include: David Beason, Monongahela, National Forest; Charles Putnam, Mark Twain, National Forest; and the keen crew in Delta National Forest, Alvin Womack, Gene Sirmon, Bruce Macko, John Strom, and Nell Anderson; and Gilbert B. Churchill, the impressive planning officer for the Monongahela.

Large selection management companies that welcomed us to their lands are Wilmon Timberlands, of Alabama; Leon Neel's operations, Georgia; Menasha Corporation, of Michigan; Pioneer Forest, of Missouri; Deltic Farms and Properties, of Arkansas; and Gibbs Brothers and Sutton Brothers, of Texas.

PATRONS

These patrons, by their substantial donations, have made it possible to include the color plates in this book without the necessity of increasing the price:

DALLAS COUNTY AUDUBON SOCIETY
KATHERINE GOODBAR
CHARLOTTE MONTGOMERY
DR. LOUIS AND PAT PARADIES
DAN REDWINE
GEORGE RUSSELL
HARDY AND BETTY SANDERS
WRAY CHARITABLE TRUST, HOUSTON

Introduction

Clearcutting most of the available commercial timber in a forest commits blasphemy upon our natural heritage.

For at least ten thousand years, America was composed of vast native forests interspersed with prairie, wetland, desert, and tundra. In the East, in addition to the mighty chestnut, there were mixed stands of Sugar maple, Tulip poplar, Black cherry, and ten kinds of oaks and hickories. In addition, the American chestnut was generally the dominant tree, but the European chestnut blight has practically extinguished the American chestnut.

In the Southeast coastal plain, American beech, Southern magnolia, and Loblolly pine grew alongside each other on the slopes, while Longleaf pine soared above Turkey oak, Bluejack oak, and tall grasses on the ridges and many of the moist flatlands, especially within a hundred miles of the Atlantic Ocean and Gulf of Mexico. The further the site from salt water, the more frequent on the uplands were shortleaf pines. In abandoned river channels, Baldcypress, Overcup oak, and Swamp chestnut oak reached gigantic proportions.

See Color Plate 26.

In the West, Douglas-fir often grew side by side with Western hemlock and Western cedar. Ponderosa pine loomed above Blue spruce, currants and cinquefoil. A tremendous diversity of animal life matched each plant community.

See photo "Ethereal Old Growth."

These biosystems were vigorous because of the interplay, symbiotic, competitive, and genetic, among the species and among individuals within each species, across extensive bioregions.

In the last two centuries, humans have opened huge gaps in these native forests, endangering the Longleaf pine/tallgrass com-

"Ethereal Old Growth," Olympic National Forest, Washington, 1988. By Trygve Steen.

In this unusual picture, the massive Western hemlock and Douglasfir at the left, 200 feet tall, appear to be floating on air. Rime on the closer branches causes the illusion. Clearcutting has reduced old-growth in the Pacific Northwest down to about two million acres.

Plate 1

Plate 2

Plate 3

Plate 4

Plate 5

Plate 6

Plate 7

Plate 8

Plate 9

Plate 10

Plate 11

Plate 12

Plate 13

Plate 14

Plate 15

Plate 16

Plate 17

Plate 18

Plate 19

Plate 20

Plate 21

Plate 22

Plate 23

Plate 24

Plate 25

Plate 26

Plate 28

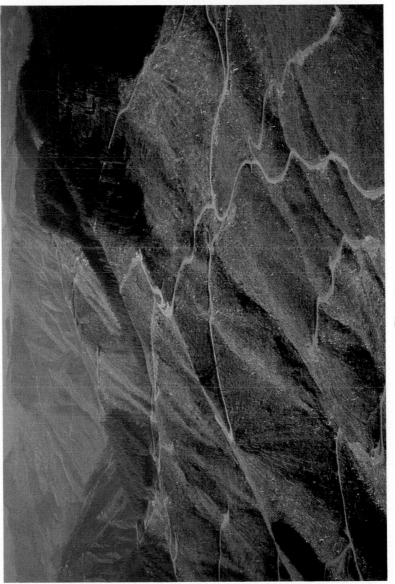

Plate 27

Plate 29

Plate 30

munity, the beech/magnolia association, and others. But almost a billion acres of woodlands remain in the United States. Five hundred million acres are commercial timberland, much of which still approximates the diversity of the native forests. The species can still relate.

In the last few decades, through a mechanized menace called "clearcutting," loggers on public and private lands have been fragmenting the native forests, disrupting the interplay between species and genetic flow within species, and desecrating our native diversity.

When they clearcut, loggers fell most of the trees in a group and move the saleable logs to market. Workers then level the remaining vegetation with bulldozers, chainsaws, chemicals, or fire. Often they leave some scattered trees for reseeding, or a string of them for such wildlife as may survive among a miserably thin strand of cover.

A clearcut looks like a war zone. It is the radical surgery of the timber business. The soil washes off like blood.

Clearcutting destroys the nests, roosts, and feeding grounds of animals of the deep forest. It kills outright the wildlife that cannot escape, including the smaller, slower animals and even the newborn of faster animals like birds and deer.

After the cutting, the landowners regrow for future clearcutting the species that bring the best prices. In some areas they plant seedlings. In others, they rely on sprouts that shoot up from stumps, roots, or fallen seeds. They cut, burn, or poison the species that compete with their commercial crop. Eventually, they have tree plantations. Native plants and animals of the deep forest never regain their former numbers. Some never come back at all.

There is a better way to produce at least as great a quantity and quality of forest products — selection management. Keville Larson, an eminent consulting forester in Mobile, Alabama, calls it "managing natural stands." Many foresters use it. We are asking Congress to direct our federal agencies to implement individual selection silviculture on whatever public lands we cannot save from being logged at all. National Audubon Society, The Wilderness Society, and Environmental Policy Institute, along with a network of smaller groups, have endorsed this concept.

CAPTIONS FOR COLOR PHOTOGRAPHS

TWO SYSTEMS OF LOGGING

A. CLEARCUTS FROM COAST TO COAST.
(Executed by private purchasers from the U.S. Forest Service)

Plate 1. George Washington National Forest (NF), Virginia (northwestern), 1987. By Brad Moore.

Loggers of the trees that were clearcut off this Appalachian mountainside left no trees, but only road-scars, where a year before had towered White oak, Sugar maple, and straight White pine. A few sprouts are beginning to restore a little foliage to the barren scape.

Plate 2. Monongahela NF, West Virginia (northeastern), 1987. By Brad Moore.

Mature White pine and mixed hardwood trees once covered this stand where only a few sticks now have life. The Forest Service will plant White pine, only, in the hope of a higher income from that commercially profitable species. This is near the spot where Sen. Jennings Randolph declared the 1970's war on clearcutting, which we lost.

Plate 3. Apalachicola NF, Florida (northeastern), 1987.

About a year after the clearcut, the Forest Service has had the area bulldozed. No stumps are visible. They have planted only Longleaf pine where once Turkey oaks under the tall Longleafs provided acorns for wildlife nourishment, and hundreds of plants flowered where now the broomsedge reigns.

Plate 4. Chattahoochee NF, Georgia (northwestern), 1987.

Twenty years after being clearcut, these oak saplings have reached the pole stage. One big tree formerly occupied this space (note stump on left). Now, nobody comes here to do anything (except to complain), much less to enjoy a walk or picnic. A clearcut is of even less value to most wild game after it reaches the pole stage than beforehand.

Plate 5. Cherokee NF, Tennessee (southeastern), 1987.

Here on the western slopes of the Appalachian Range, the clearcuts look about the same as everywhere else. Some White pines are making headway, but it will be decades before this stand has much value for any purpose. Meanwhile tons of soil and nutrients have eroded off this steep slope.

Plate 6. Hoosier NF, Indiana (southern), 1987. By Brad Moore.

Clearcutters didn't leave a sign of life here in the infamous Little Africa grove, where runaway slaves once rested in the forest en route northward to freedom. In the background, Tulip poplar and Red maple are populating an earlier clearcut.

Plate 7. Delta NF, Mississippi (western), 1987. By Brad Moore.

The clearcutters left a few big culls like the Green ash in the foreground, but the Forest Service sent men with hypo-spears to kill them, so that Nuttall oaks would dominate the scene. Oaks bring a better price. The ring of small openings about a foot above the ground is where the spears injected poison into the cambium. Sometimes, hulks like these will struggle on for years before succumbing. Poison is an alternative to bulldozing as the second step in a clearcut — all to remove competitors of higher-priced trees.

Plate 8. Mark Twain NF, Missouri (southeast), 1987. By Brad Moore.

The timber purchaser has removed the Shortleaf pines and most of the White oaks, leaving a few of the latter for the use of whatever wildlife may venture into a clearcut. Some White oak sprouts in the foreground are springing up from the only parts of felled trees that remain — the roots.

Plate 9. Chequamegon NF, Wisconsin (northwestern), 1978.

Here, the Forest Service sells the forest conifers and hardwoods under the clearcut method to open the field for Quaking aspen. After a few decades they sell the aspen ("poppel") to be clearcut for paper pulp. This is a switch on the usual replacement of other trees by conifers. Here, aspen grow faster and bring in the most dollars. The ruts indicate the greater compaction caused by the heavier equipment used in clearcutting.

Plate 10. Ouachita NF, Arkansas (west central), 1987.

On thin rocky soil of the Ouachita Mountains, all species grow slowly. Nevertheless, the Forest Service sells timber at age eighty or one hundred for clearcutting and starting over. They plant Shortleaf pine on south-facing and west-facing slopes. Even there, erosion is fierce. Shortleafs will seldom attain the size of the previous stand (note Shortleafs on the right). In the Ouachita, Forest Service personnel often suppress hardwoods by prescribed burning, as they did to prepare this site for pine seedlings.

Plate 11. Sam Houston NF, Texas (southeastern), 1984. Bv James Jackson.

Imagine the gall of a bureaucracy that would wipe out an area like this, setting back the stand for eighty years, and the native diversity forever, so that nobody could enjoy the place for half a century, and yet leave a sign there like this one! In southern pine forests, the agency follows up such devastation by planting pines and conducting a series of burns that permit the young pines to grow on, but suppress all other species.

Plate 12. Arapaho NF, Colorado (central), 1982.

Several years after a clearcut, the young Douglas-firs are struggling, but will never grow enough to recover the high cost of regenerating them on this high Rocky Mountain ridge. In this region, as most, the Forest Service spends more on raising a crop than it gets back by selling it.

Plate 13. Mendocino NF, California (west central), 1982. By Patrick Carr.

In an attempt to avoid stirring up the powerful environmental movement in San Francisco, the Forest Service did not launch full-scale clearcutting in this forest a few hours north until 1982. But since then, it has been degrading many a fine recreational area, as in this ridge-top clearcut, to expose the mineral soil for Douglas-fir seeding.

Plate 14. Siskiyou NF, Oregon (southwestern), 1986.

This clearcut squats only 200 yards below the trailhead to Babyfoot Lake, marring the purity of that previously unlogged area. Visible in the background is the inevitable road that enables cable equipment and hauling trucks to come and go through areas like this that environmentalists have proposed for wilderness legislation.

Plate 15. Olympic NF, Washington (northwestern), 1987.

The Forest Service is clearcutting to the borders of Olympic National Park, making that sanctified ground an island in a sea of barrens like this one. In this northern clime, even a year or two after the clearcut, there was little sign of vegetation.

Plate 16. Tongass NF, Alaska (southeast), 1986. By J. Warren.

Here on Chichagof Island and throughout this sixteen million acre forest, the Forest Service makes clearcut sales for $2 per thousand board feet, only a percent or two of the cost to the Forest Service. Two timber companies have fifty-year contracts for all timber sold, which they resell primarily to the Orient. These clearcuts are entirely in old growth timber, sacking the native diversity, eroding the soil, and silting the streams that must remain clear for salmon to spawn. The Tongass bill in Congress would reduce the logging and permit free-market pricing, but would not restrain the Forest Service from using the clearcutting system.

B. SELECTION FORESTS FROM COAST TO COAST.

Plate 17. Wilmon Timberlands, Inc., Alabama (south central), 1987. By Brad Moore.

In these 55,000 acres, foresters combine a successful timber business with recreation, wildlife, and preservation of native diversity. Many plant associations thrive, including White oak/Southern red oak/Loblolly pine as depicted here. These stands contain trees of all ages and all species native to this part of Alabama.

Plate 18.   Leon Toliver's Woods, Indiana (southern), 1987. By Brad Moore.

A jeweler and his wife, with no prior education or experience in forestry, but with a forester's guidance, are managing their own woods for timber sales every seven or ten years, including White oak, Red oak, Sugar maple, and White ash. They let all species survive here, including Serviceberry (in flower on left) and American beech (on right). Wherever they have created an opening (by selling a tree or two), scores of seedlings are springing up in natural regeneration, a hallmark of selection management.

Plate 19.   Tom Thompson's Woods, Illinois (southern), 1987. By Brad Moore.

Northern red oak and Southern red oak mingle with the other species of tree, shrub, and forb of the region in this single-tree selection stand. The stump in the right foreground will soon be obscured by all the young trees that are surging upward.

Plate 20.   Menasha Corporation, Michigan (southwestern), 1988. By Randall L. Kuipers.

In this stand of many species (including Black cherry), stumps indicate that Menasha's foresters marked and purchased trees that were close to trees with straight, limbless trunks, leaving the latter for a subsequent harvest. That is why selection cutting is often called improvement cutting.

Plate 21.   Wolf Springs Forest, Wisconsin (northwestern), 1984. By Charles H. Stoddard.

After one hundred years of selection management by him and predecessors, "Chuck" Stoddard, author of a forestry text, still manages his Red pine/White pine forest under individual-tree selection. The narrow road winding among the trees illustrates how selection managers respect the natural appearance of their stands while saving excessive road-building costs. Stoddard leases part of this forest to Boy Scouts and others for recreation use.

Plate 22.   Pioneer Forest, Missouri (southeastern), 1987. By Brad Moore.

Here, commercial species such as Southern red oak and Shortleaf pine dominate many of the Ozark hills, and deer and turkey thrive. St. Louis benefactor Leo Drey does not have to make a killing out of his 153,000 acres of timberland, so he and Clinton Trammell, his chief forester, manage the land for native diversity, as well as for timber. It turns out that selection management serves both purposes feasibly.

Plate 23. Deltic Farms and Timberlands, Arkansas (central), 1988. By James Norman.

This stand features Shortleaf pine, Black oak, Southern red oak, and Mockernut hickory, of all ages. Further south in Arkansas, Deltic's forests are predominantly Loblolly pine, White oak, and Sweet gum. Deltic's 400,000 acres are mostly in selection management. That system has proven to produce better profits because it saves the high costs of artificial regeneration — bulldozing and tree-planting.

Plate 24. Gibbs Brothers, Texas (southeastern), 1988.

For forty years this family enterprise has been restoring cut-over pine/hardwood stands to beautiful, profitable forests by means of selection management. Note the deer stand. Hunting leases bring in extra profits. Of 55,000 acres, all but 5,000 are mainly in Shortleaf and Loblolly pine, but the foresters save whatever species can survive periodic prescribed burning, which is most of them.

Plate 25. David Parker's Woods, Oregon (western), 1988. By David Parker.

A number of small landowners are doing what some pundits claim cannot be done — selection management of Douglasfir on steep slopes. A problem is felling huge trees without damaging too many others. The solution is to use care. It is being done, as depicted here.

C. OLD GROWTH, MULTIPLE CLEARCUTS, TURKEYS, AND ENDANGERED SPECIES.

Plate 26. McGee Bend, Angelina NF, Texas (southeastern), 1988. By Larry Shelton.

This old-growth grove of more than 100 acres in a river bend of 1,000 acres contains Baldcypress (one exceeds twenty-five feet in circumference), Overcup oak, Swamp chestnut oak, Willow oak, Water hickory, Black gum, and Water tupelo. McGee Bend is subject to clearcutting. The Forest Service has scheduled no sale in 1989. Texas Committee on Natural Resources is asking the Forest Service to designate McGee Bend as a research natural area. Except for a few thousand acres, all the unprotected old-growth in the national forests is west of the Great Plains. McGee Bend escaped the saw around the turn of the century because the Angelina River was in flood when a timber company logged the general area.

Plate 27. Seven clearcuts, Santiam Watershed, Willamette NF, Oregon (west central), 1988. By Diane Kelsay.

Native diversity in a large area might survive a single small clearcut, but when an agency clearcuts stand after stand, as is the practice, it fragments the habitat to the extent that many of the native species vanish throughout the large area. That is the situation in the Santiam, where the Spotted owl, Red vole, Pine Marten, Fisher, and Wolverine and associated species are on the way out.

Plate 28. Ten Clearcuts, Jefferson NF, Virginia (southwestern), 1987. By Brad Moore.

All across the nation, the Forest Service (and other federal agencies with timberland) are selling timber for clearcuts separated by small (as here) or larger buffers. This shatters an outing for a forest-lover. What is even worse, after the new plantations grow ten feet high, the Forest Service generally comes back and sells the trees in the buffers for clearcutting. After a rotation (70–120 years), almost all the available commercial timber is in even-age stands of one or two species that bring the highest sale prices.

Plate 29. Red-cockaded woodpecker at its nesting cavity, Angelina NF, Texas (southeastern), 1988. By Mildred and Leon Ladyman.

The bird characteristically flecked off the outer bark until resin flowed near the hole, apparently discouraging snakes, because they do not like resin on their scales. In 1988, U.S. District Judge Robert M. Parker, after hearing all the evidence on both sides, ordered the U.S. Forest Service to shift from clearcutting to selection management in all habitat zones of the Red-cockaded woodpecker in four national forests (total acreage, 200,000) because clearcutting was further jeopardizing this endangered species.

Plate 30. "Tink" Smith Forest, West Virginia (eastern), 1988. By Glenn C. Smith.

Unlike the Rio Grande wild turkey, the Eastern wild turkey inhabits tall forests. "Tink" Smith finds numerous individuals on his minimally logged 500 acres, alternating between the deepest and the openest parts. Wildlife managers disagree on the extent to which Eastern wild turkeys need a closed canopy forest, but most authorities agree that these birds were here when the eastern forest was almost unbroken except by rivers. That was before the advent of humans. Few would contend that turkeys need any more clearcutting than has already been done.

PART I

A Look at Mayhem

WHAT CLEARCUTTING IS AND DOES

From coast to clearcut coast, government and industry are wiping out the wild plant and animal habitats that our ancestors enjoyed and relied upon for survival, and that we still need in many ways. They are clearcutting away the native diversity in our forests and replacing it with commercial tree farms. Our grandchildren will be shorn of a vast gene-pool for new medicines, resistant foods and fibers, and adequate living laboratories where we can continue to utilize nature and also to enjoy it.

Clearcutting wipes out almost all life aboveground and much belowground.

It is like performing brain surgery with a meat-cleaver.

Its apologists call the system "even-age management." We call it "clearcutting," for three reasons:

1. The term, "clearcutting" is better known.
2. It is shorter.
3. It does not euphemize the harsh reality of devastation.

Clearcutting is the roughest way to manage timberland.

Technically speaking, clearcutting is the felling of all trees in a group in one operation. We also use the term to cover two-step clearing and all the measures that clearcutters take to eradicate all

1

species that compete with their chosen ones. (See Glossary at back of book.) We could call it "even-age mismanagement," a tool of even-age man.

Clearcutting involves the deliberate eradication of natural life systems, the decimation of some species, and the disruption of genetic diversity — even within the chosen species — all to make a quick profit from the largest trees cut and to raise crops of a fast-growing strain in their place.

Logging need not involve this gene-ocide. Foresters can, and many private operators do, raise and sell diverse tree species at a profit with a system that inflicts far less insult on the earth. That system is individual-tree selection.

The motivation for wholesale (forest-wide) clearcutters is a larger margin of profit. They overlook several factors:

1. Their calculations are short-term, ignoring the long-run decline in soil and nutrients and therefore the eventual decline in growth that clearcutting spawns.
2. They do not include in their cost figures losses to native wildlife, diversity, and recreation.
3. They calculate on the net present value method. Under the more realistic cost efficiency method, selection management excels.
4. An antiquated law enables them to funnel more funds into the Forest Service budget when they clearcut.

In 1894, Congress started the national forest system as a vast set of reserves for future resource needs, as open spaces for public recreation, and as storage and filtration areas for our public waters. There are now 190 million acres under the Forest Service (FS), about half those acres are commercial timberlands. Congress authorized similar purposes for lands of the Bureau of Land Management (BLM) and Bureau of Indian Affairs (BIA). The Armed Services also have forested lands. These agencies have authority to sell timber under stated methods to private loggers. Since 1964, the method has been predominantly clearcutting. The National Park Service cannot sell its forests.

EXTENT OF CLEARCUTTING

With devastating effects, federal agencies are sentencing almost all their available timber land to be clearcut during the next one hundred years. (See Table 1) This acreage is one-fifth of all the commercial timberland in the United States. The agencies that sell logs have been clearcutting nationwide since 1964, and plan to have clearcut almost one hundred million acres at least once within the rotation period of 60 to 120 years. They go after the best part first, the old-growth forests.

TABLE 1

Federal Agency	Acres clearcut or vulnerable to clearcutting (in millions)
Forest Service (lower 48)	80
Forest Service (Alaska)	2
Bureau of Land Management	4
Bureau of Indian Affairs	1
U.S. Fish & Wildlife Service	1
Military	2 *
Total	90

*Difficult to ascertain. The Army and Air Force say that they sell timber only when they do not need their forests for military activities. A vast majority of the commercial harvests on their timber is by clearcutting.

As required by the National Forest Management Act of 1976, the Forest Service has issued fifty-year resource management plans for most of the national forests. They call for continued "even-age management" of virtually all the available commercial timber.

Meanwhile, most of the industrial timber raisers (e.g. Weyerhauser, Wesvaco, Champion-International, and St. Regis) are clearcutting their huge landholdings.

In the absence of strong state forestry laws for private lands, there is little we can do about the private clearcutting, though other citizen groups are waging hard fights in states like California and Oregon.

However, on the federal level we can utilize a legal and political system effectively for major overhaul of the current system. It will require a unified national effort.

STRATEGY — AMEND NFMA, OVERHAUL THE BUREAUCRACIES

In 1976, when Congress enacted the National Forest Management Act (NFMA), citizen groups were divided. As a result, the FS and timber industry were able to insert loopholes in the provisions relating to clearcutting and diversity. With better education and coordination today, citizens could influence Congress to close those loopholes, and could elect a President who will overhaul the top echelons of the FS and BLM.

Some groups have adopted these goals: to substitute individual-tree selection, to require preservation of native diversity, to save all remaining old-growth, and to reform the bureaucracies. Other citizens have aims that are less comprehensive, or more so.

The sooner we unite and prevail, the less of Mother Earth we will lose to clearcutting.

LOOK HOMEWARD, ANGEL!

Many of the stands being clearcut contain temperate ecosystems rich in native diversity. Among the oldest and biggest of the condemned trees, old-growth Douglas-firs and Western hemlocks in the Pacific Northwest frequently exceed even the largest tropical forest trees in height, girth, and age. Even in the East, there remain old stands of smaller trees.

Many authors, with good cause, have alerted Americans to the disastrous clearcutting of tropical forests. It is time that we recognize also that Americans are fast destroying our own forests. We need to save both tropical and temperate forests, but we have more power to save our own federal forests because we have more of a voice in our own government than in other international and foreign institutions.

WE HAVE TO ACT FAST!

In most of the country, the loggers have already clearcut about one-fourth of the federal commercial timber, meaning the marketable stands not protected as Wilderness, or deferred for recreation, scenic, natural, or other purposes. Only seventeen percent of the land in our National Forests has been designated Wilderness. Most of this Wilderness was not marketable for timber harvest anyhow, because it is lake, desert, above timber line, or otherwise unproductive for growing wood.

The clearcutters harvest a stand at the end of the rotation period. In the Pacific Northwest, the rotation period for Douglas-fir stands is usually one hundred years, as in the Appalachians, for oak and cherry. Every year, the government sells about one percent of such timberlands to private timber companies to be clearcut. From Texas to North Carolina, the rotation of Loblolly pine is usually seventy years, so the annual sales exceed one percent. This process has been going on since 1964 (even earlier in the Pacific Northwest). As of 1988, around twenty-five percent of the available stands in most regions have been clearcut.

To save the rest, fast action is needed.
See photo "Clearcutting on a Rampage."

THE ANATOMY OF A CLEARCUT

Prior to a logging operation, the involved agency has a road built to the site. The last leg of the logging road is often cut through prime forest. Next, loggers saw down the trees that the agency has sold. In a clearcut sale, the falling trees mash the soil and understory vegetation. On steep slopes, loggers often cable or high-line the sawlogs (drag or carry them by cable). Elsewhere, using heavy-wheeled machines, called skidders, they usually skid the logs to a "landing," where they stack the logs for pick-up and hauling. Skidding compacts the soil and remaining vegetation, and often leaves ruts. The agency sees no reason to spare anything, because it looks upon native vegetation as an obstacle to the growing of a commercial species.

Big trucks equipped with loading gear soon arrive. Workers load the sawlogs and haul them to the mills, leaving a scene of stark desolation — shredded snags and uprooted brush and slash among patches of bare earth. It looks like a war zone. During rains, sheet erosion is rampant, causing gulleys to form. Topsoil is lost.

COMPLETING THE KILL

The next step is to get the stumps, slash, brush and snags out of the way in order to expose soil for starting commercial seedlings. They euphemistically label this process, "site preparation." Most commercial seedlings start best in open sunlight on bare soil.

In Central Oregon forests, Forest Service workers or contractors often bulldoze the slash, or on steep slopes cable the stumps and heavy refuse into piles. They generally burn the piles with the aid of diesel fuel.

In the Gulf Coastal Plain and many other regions, particularly on flat lands, they use heavy equipment to shear off all the dead,

"Clearcutting on a Rampage." Flathead NF, Montana (northwestern), 1988. By James R. Conner.

To show numerous clearcuts, aerial photography is best. Here, on Crane Mountain, the Forest Service has already clearcut close to a hundred units, fragmenting the forest almost beyond enjoyment by humans and beyond survival by some species of wildlife. In response to a citizen appeal, the Chief of the forest Service has stated that Congress left a lot of discretion in the agency when it called for maintenance of diversity in the National Forest Management Act. The agency has stretched that discretion.

dying, and surviving vegetation near or below ground level, including roots and stumps, and to shove it into windrows.

See photo "Site Preparation Equipment."

In eastern national forests from the Ouachita N.F. in Arkansas and Oklahoma to George Washington N.F. in Virginia, particularly on rocky slopes, the Forest Service has used herbicides as a part of site preparation for subsequent "pine-planting." They often inject the poison into the cambium of surviving trees.

See Color Plate 7.

After site prep, the agencies usually abandon the clearcut for up to five years. In that period, weeds, sprouts and wild seedlings spring up.

See Color Plates 3 and 8.

SEED TREE AND SHELTERWOOD

In a small fraction of harvests in many regions, the timber agencies leave scattered trees of the preferred species to reseed the stand. They call this "seed tree" cutting if they leave five to ten trees per acre, and "shelterwood" cutting if they leave roughly twice as many. Even using these two methods, they generally bulldoze or chainsaw all vegetation except the seed trees, to open up for the preferred seedlings. Shelterwood is becoming the usual cutting method in the Green Mountain N.F. of Vermont and the Allegheny N.F. in Pennsylvania. As soon as enough seedlings are thriving, the Forest Service sells the "mother" trees. Loggers drive right through the seedlings, saw down the "mother" trees, and haul them to the mill.

So far as aesthetics, soil, and wildlife are concerned, these two-stage "clearcuts" are slightly preferable to one-stage cuts, but still suffer all the disadvantages of one-stage clearcuts, particularly the loss of native diversity.

"REGENERATION"

After clearcuts on hardwood sites, from Wisconsin's aspen stands and the Ozarks of Missouri to the Appalachians of the East, the Forest Service generally lets the more profitable species regenerate naturally from the stumps, roots, and seeds left behind.

On other sites, comprising the great majority of sawlogs, forest managers grow a crop of a single preferred species of tree, the most

"Site Preparation Equipment," George Washington NF, Virginia (western), 1987.
Parked here between forays into a past clearcut, this machine can mount a blade as a "pusher" or haul a chopper to dispose of all remaining vegetation. Ernie Dickerman, of Virginia, the great pro-wilderness lobbyist, and Charlie Jamieson the skilled conservationist-pilot, take a look at the wheels, which compact the soil increasingly during an operation.

profitable kind. In the Pacific Northwest, the usual crop is Doug-las-fir. In the Southeast, it is Loblolly or Shortleaf pine. Usually, instead of relying on nature to come up with the tree that can grow there the best, the foresters raise in nurseries the seedlings of one species, and have them planted by hand or machine.

They call them "superior trees" because the seeds come from "desired" stock. Many scientists believe that this genetic diversion by foresters may reduce native diversity within a species and there-fore result in less resistance to insects and diseases, and less flexi-bility to adapt to changing conditions.

PINE-CLONING

In almost every stand of seedlings, numerous species form a dense thicket competing with the "preferred" trees. The intrepid foresters have an arsenal of weapons to attack these competitors. In the Ouachita National Forest workers often spray herbicides by hand on all but the pines.

In the East and Southeast, the Forest Service often orders ground crews to cut the "brush" or operators of heavy equipment to weave through the stand, shearing mainly "undesirable spe-cies." When the pines are about twenty feet tall, the foresters begin a series of prescribed burns. With the aid of diesel torches, they burn the vegetation to a height of five or ten feet. This deadens most of the oaks, hickories, elms, and other hardwood trees and shrubs that have sprouted in the stand. Most hardwood species do not grow as fast as the young pines, and are not as resistant to fire.

The Forest Service and other agencies repeatedly attack the surviving competitors by girdling, hypo-hatcheting, or spraying herbicides by truck or by air. They call this "timber stand improve-ment." The result is a virtual timber monoculture in each managed stand.

For decades the stand is a dense thicket of skinny poles. Then the foresters perform a series of thinnings. They cut some of the preferred species, and more of the other species, if any still survive.

CUTTING SURGEONS

In its wholesale clearcutting, the Forest Service is like a "cut-ting surgeon" who amputates limbs from every wounded person brought to the hospital. Worse than that, the Forest Service goes out looking for healthy forests and amputates them.

True, it plants new trees; but what it plants are of one species, like Loblolly pine in the South in place of the oaks, hickories, pines and gums, or Douglas-fir in the Northwest, instead of spruces, firs, and a myriad of other species that it amputates. That is like executing large groups of people and replacing them with clones of a different strain produced in a laboratory. It is gene-ocide.

THE LUCKY FEW

The bureaucrats do not carry out this entire clearcutting process in all stands in all regions. Around Los Angeles and San Diego, the Forest Service does not clearcut at all, because the area is too dry to grow another stand of trees within a millenium, and because the well-organized outdoor lovers of that area would raise bloody hell if they saw a clearcut.

The Forest Service faces similar deterrents in the Uinta National Forest in the mountains overlooking the Salt Lake City-Provo urban complex. In Mendocino National Forest north of San Francisco, they restrained their clearcutting until recent years.

In national forests on the coastal plain of the Gulf of Mexico, the Forest Service clearcuts up to 100% of all hardwood and mixed stands, as well as pine stands. Early on, the "timber beasts" in the Forest Service designated all hardwood or hardwood/pine types as pine types if they would sustain pines in commercial quantities. The few stands (about 6%) that the FS acknowledges as hardwood types regenerate as best they can, which is often about 50% to pine, since pine takes advantage of the vast exposure to sunlight in clearcuts.

One national forest in this region is totally hardwood, the Delta N.F. in Mississippi. Here, they favor Nuttall oak, a sun-loving species, by using all three versions of clearcutting.

PART II

The Bad Seeds

SAPPING THE GENE POOLS OF OUR
NATURAL HERITAGE

See photo "Glory primeval."

Clearcutting disrupts native diversity of life systems, species, and genes within species. Fortunately, about fifty millions of acres of native life systems remain in our federal timberlands despite programs to convert them into assembly lines. The agencies haven't yet sold most of their timber for clearcutting. About twenty million acres of the unsold stands are old-growth, the dynamic communities of trees greater than 150 years of age that were prevalent when humans first ventured onto this continent. Our remaining old-growth forests, mostly in Oregon, Washington and Alaska, are the most valuable treasures that public agencies threaten to destroy.

Also on a few bottomlands in the South and East, there are federal commercial timberlands that have never been harvested. The amount of unprotected federal old-growth forest remaining is 2.6 million acres in Washington-Oregon, fifteen million in Alaska, and about two million scattered in small acreages elsewhere. This does not include inventoried roadless areas under temporary restrictions as potential wildernesses.

See photo "Mill Creek Cove."

12

"Glory Primeval," Siskiyou NF, Oregon (southwestern), 1988. By Trygve Steen.
    Sunrise through the fog over Indian Creek creates an impression of the inchoate. This is a forest of dynamic stability. At lengthy intervals, lightning starts big fires, but in another 100 years or so, after several stages of succession, the Douglas-fir and the hemlock once again "stand like Druids of old." Modern clearcutting, with its site preparation and cloneplanting, totally disrupts this natural process. Citizen groups have proposed a North Kalmiopsis National Park to stop clearcutting in the southern Siskiyou.

"Mill Creek Cove," Sabine NF, Texas, 1978. By Christopher Runk.
      *These 90 acres of beech/magnolia forest, never cut, constitute the largest
remaining old-growth stand of this vegetation association, designated as threatened in
Texas. In this climate, American beech generally rot and fall by age 200, but the
Southern magnolias, up to more than 13 feet in circumference and 120 feet tall, live on
for centuries longer. For a depiction of this Scenic Area in words and color, see*
Realms of Beauty, University of Texas Press, 1984, by Edward C. Fritz
and Jess Alford.

Also some timberlands have grown back from logging early in this century or in the 1800's and have retained most of their pre-logging life systems. Not all of the early logging was by clearcutting. Even where it was clearcut, the loggers in the old days permitted the natural vegetation to restore itself after the cut. The native hardwoods returned from roots, stumps, and seeds. Loggers did not bulldoze nor poison the remaining vegetation, nor plant pines, nor burn repeatedly to suppress non-commercial species, as the bureaucrats are doing today.

In the old days, even the clearcut-and-get-outers did not commit gene-ocide to the extent that the bureaucrats do today.

Today, wherever they clearcut, the bureaucrats extirpate a native plant association.

See photo "Sterile Forest."

Clearcutters, private and federal, have reduced the beech/magnolia association of the South so drastically that the Society of American Foresters has removed it from its listing of forest types.

Clearcutting and its attendant commercialization have also endangered the Longleaf pine/tallgrass community of Gulf Coastal Plain states from Virginia south to Florida and west to Texas because Longleafs cannot be planted successfully, do not resprout in a clearcut, and have a much slower above-ground growth rate than the commercially preferred Loblolly and Slash pines. The Florida Natural Areas Inventory recognizes Longleaf/Wiregrass as a threatened plant association. Although degraded Longleaf sandhill communities still occupy much of Florida, high quality examples are almost non-existent.

Along with the diversity of overstory, modern clearcutting demolishes the middle story species like Eastern hophornbeam, Eastern dogwood, and Swamp red maple in the South; and Oregon ash, Bigleaf maple, and Red alder in the Northwest. Some individuals come back after the cut, only to be suppressed during the pole stage of the plantation process.

See Table Two. This table is, perforce, incomplete. For some areas, data on original forest composition is lacking; and within given regions, associations are highly variable.

According to Dr. Peter Raven, of Missouri, almost every tree species is ecologically linked with some twenty or thirty other plant species. For example, beechdrop is a flowering plant that obtains nutrients from the roots of the beech. When the beech is eliminated,

"Sterile Forest," Angelina NF, Texas (southeastern), 1976.
    This 20-year old pine planation contains nothing else except a few sprigs of grass. Ironically, it stands about 100 feet behind a Forest Service monument, "Magnolia Forest." Two magnolia trees grow beside the sign. They are all the magnolias in that vicinity.

TABLE TWO

LOSS OF PLANT COMMUNITY WHEN CLEARCUT
(From Coast to Coast)

Dominant Trees of Native Plant Association	Replacement	Area
Sitka spruce/Incense cedar/Western hemlock	Sitka spruce	W. Washington
Port Orford cedar/Western hemlock/Douglas-fir	Douglas-fir	S.W. Oregon
Western cedar/Ponderosa pine/Sugar pine	Ponderosa pine	N. California
Jack pine/Black spruce/White spruce/Aspen	Aspen	Minnesota
Hemlock/Sugar maple/Red pine/White pine/Aspen	Aspen	N.W. Wisconsin
Beech/S. Magnolia/Loblolly pine/White oak	Loblolly pine	East Texas
S. Red oak/Shortleaf pine/Mockernut hickory	Shortleaf pine	Cent. Arkansas
Loblolly pine/Shortleaf pine/S. Red oak/Pignut	Loblolly pine	W. Mississippi
Red maple/Black cherry/Whiteoak/Black oak/Mockernut hickory	Black Cherry or White oak	Missouri
Northern red oak/Sugar maple/Chestnut oak	N. red oak	Indiana
White pine/Sugar maple/Red oak	White pine	E. Tennessee
Spruce pine/American elm/Nuttall oak	Nuttall oak	Alabama
White oak/Loblolly pine/Black gum	Loblolly pine	N. Florida
Longleaf pine/Turkey oak/Wire grass	Slash pine	E. Florida
Sugar maple/White oak/Black cherry	Black cherry	Virginia

the beechdrop vanishes also. Some species, such as the alders and legumes, can take nitrogen from the air and fix it into usable form which enriches the soil when the leaves and twigs fall. Without these nitrogen-fixers, the soil loses fertility. Clearcutting reduces the abundance of nitrogen-fixers. In the Pacific Northwest, alder is one of the pioneer species, but the Forest Service sprays herbicides to kill it.

Clearcutting also destroys the understory shrubbery and ground cover that require deep shade. In Alaska, one of these species is bunchberry, an important element in the diet of Sitka black-tailed deer. When bunchberries diminish, the deer diminish.

Below the groundcover swarm thousands of species of insects, nematodes, worms, unicellular plants and animals, viruses, and fungi. They make the soil rich. Some of them, including certain fungi, supply nutrients to roots of trees and flowering plants, and draw photosynthesized energy from those trees and flowers in return. Douglas-fir and certain other conifers take up nutrients and water efficiently only if mycorrhiza fungi grow on their roots. Clearcutting reduces these soil organisms by compaction, exposure, erosion, overheating from prescribed burns, and elimination of roots on which to feed.

See photo "Mark of Vengeance."

A natural ecosystem links a huge network of species interacting in multiple ways. It is metastable, capable of rebounding from such major perturbations as forest fires, insect attacks, and harsh weather. For instance, Lodgepole pine forests of the Rocky Mountains, before the days of fire suppression by the Forest Service, would bounce back after crown fires every 300 to 400 years, (Lodgepole fire cycle, Thomas Lawson, Forest Watch, November 1986.)

In the Southeast, beech and magnolia can regain their dominance after devastating hurricanes open them up to decades of invasion by pines. Such catastrophes do not destroy the roots and seeds in the ground, and do not repeat often enough to eliminate the sprouts that spring up afterwards. But once clearcut, a forest type may take centuries to regain its balance. Some systems may never return to pre-clearcut composition, especially if the ground layer has been destroyed by site preparation. If assaulted repeatedly, as in even-age management, any life system will probably never restore itself.

"Mark of Vengeance," Sam Houston NF, Texas (southeastern), 1984.

The upper photo by Brad Moore depicts the broader scene. The lower by Jess Alford is eyeball to a rut.

Before the holocaust, the richest tree-shaded fern bed in Texas covered this entire setting. On October 3, 1984, after final passage of the bill that designated Little Lake Creek as wilderness, a timber company cut and removed all the big pine trees that it had recently bought in a rush deal between it and the Forest Service to beat the President's signature on the bill. The next day, the timber company forester personally ran a bulldozer through the entire fern bed that wilderness supporters had long acclaimed. A few months earlier, that forester had been the Forest Service ranger in charge of this area. He had strongly opposed the wilderness bill, as had the entire Forest Service. Then he had reached retirement age and kept up the struggle on behalf of the timber company.

Human beings depend for survival on native life systems. These systems have developed the genetic strengths from which we derived and continue to bolster most of our foods and fibers, and many medicines, and other products. As our domesticated grains and other foods weaken and become susceptible to insects and diseases, we must borrow from wild ecosystems to restore their genetic strength. We need those wild genes that clearcutting destroys.

In several regions where the Forestry bureaucracies are raising and planting "supertrees" all from the same stock, they use poisons to eradicate other trees of the same species. Not trusting their supertrees to outgrow wild trees, they artificially help their supertrees to compete in a plantation! This, despite the fact that a species survives by virtue of the diverse genetic compositions of its individuals. When the environment changes, some individuals can adapt while others cannot. The adapters maintain the species. By raising fields of clones, the bureaucrats reduce genetic diversity within the only surviving tree species in a stand, and thereby reduce the survivability of the species.

CLEARCUTS DECIMATE NATIVE WILDLIFE

During the cutting and site preparation phases, and during prescribed burns and chemical "treatments," the clearcutters kill not merely plants, but also thousands of animals, generally those that cannot fly or run hundreds of yards, and the newly born or eggs of more mobile animals. Lizards, turtles, frogs, armadillos, opossums, raccoons, fawns and baby birds, are crushed or burned, or killed in falls as their hole trees crash to the ground. Equally tragic, because all life depends on them, insects, worms, and smaller animals, down to the microscopic, are destroyed by the millions. Even more devastating than initial slaughter is the destruction of native habitats, because loss of habitat means the death of entire populations.

When a Sitka spruce stand is clearcut (Alaska), Sitka blacktail deer in that locality starve or freeze to death. Intensive timber harvesting of the coastal forests of Vancouver Island . . . resulted in deer population decline of 50–75%." (Technical Report 85–3, Alaska Fish and Game Dept.) The deer lose their favorite foods, like bunchberry, and their winter cover. The closed-canopy second-growth stage (age 25–50) is a virtual desert in terms of forage, even for deer.

When they clearcut an old-growth Douglas-fir/Western hemlock stand in the Pacific Northwest, Red vole, lynx, marten, and fisher vanish. The widespread Barred owl takes over from the endangered Spotted owl. The Spotted owl loses that particular population, which is a reason why Spotted owls throughout the Pacific Northwest are vanishing.

Once a stand is clearcut, some of its inhabitants never return. In Southeastern hardwoods, a clearcut, followed by a pine plantation, permanently eradicates Pileated woodpecker, Swainson's warbler, and other animals from the site, as well as Nodding Nixie and other shade-demanding plants. A clearcut also eliminates beech and its twenty or more associated species for fifty years. In a rotation of only seventy or eighty years, a fifty-year recovery period is too long for these plants to reestablish before the next clearcut.

The endangered Red-cockaded woodpecker nests mainly in live pines that are beginning to die. Therefore, it has to keep changing hole trees and colony sites. When the Forest Service clearcuts pine stands in the South near a Red-cockaded woodpecker colony, the birds often abandon that colony. (Environmental Impact Statement, Texas Forest Plan) There are no known examples of Red-cockadeds colonizing a new site. A population can survive individual-tree selection where older trees are left standing, but cannot survive wholesale clearcutting.

See Color Plate 29.

In the North, according to Technical Report 85–3 by Alaska Game and Fish Department, the new sprouts in some clearcuts will sustain moose for a while, but when the young trees reach the pole thicket stage, the moose cannot find enough food there.

In the South, Grey squirrels and Flying squirrels need numerous mature hardwood trees and cannot sustain a sizeable population in a clearcut, even where loggers leave old snags or stringers of hardwoods. Likewise, Eastern wild turkeys need large acreages of hardwoods to survive.

See Color Plate 30.

In short, clearcuts extirpate nearly all species that require closed-canopy forests. If there was an adjoining habitat suitable to such a species that was unoccupied by other members of that species, the displaced individuals might relocate. But that seldom happens. The more clearcuts that occur the fewer individuals of some species will survive.

True, other animals that do not need a deep forest will populate clearcuts — certain sparrows, grasshoppers, field rats and other occupants of openings. But these species are already common in all the other burgeoning clearcuts, pastures and fields of the human dominated landscape. A new clearcut adds no new species to the region, but further reduces species of mature forests.

The Forest Service sometimes admits to a certain amount of attrition of wildlife after clearcutting. Table IV-4 in the draft Land and Resource Management Plan for National Forests in Texas projects that the scheduled continuation of massive clearcutting for fifty years will cause the following habitat declines (in thousands of animals): squirrels, 414 to 315; turkey, 21 to 14; small game, 32 to 24; and even quail, 5.8 to 5.6. The Texas Plan even admits a drop in the endangered Red-cockaded woodpecker from 208 to 88 colonies, under scheduled clearcutting. Less biased analysts say that squirrels and turkeys would probably lose 90% or more of their habitat, and in the long-run, some species like the Red-cockaded woodpecker might disappear altogether because of separation of tiny populations from each other, and consequent genetic deterioration.

Plans for other forests, like the Monongahela in West Virginia, do not project present and subsequent populations for comparison. The Monongahela EIS, 2-46ff, compares populations of certain species under various alternatives, with the absurd conclusion that there will be fewer Wild turkey, Black bear, and Grey squirrel under selection management than under other alternatives. The EIS gives no explanation, but it probably has to do with the fact that under even-age management, the plan would arbitrarily shut down far more roads between harvests than under selection.

CLEARCUTS WRECK OUR DISPERSED RECREATION

From the day the loggers enter, for at least the next forty years, clearcuts repel visitors. There are minor exceptions — hunters of Virginia white-tailed deer who set up blinds along the surrounding edges, and bird-watchers who seek species like Prairie warblers that nest in fifteen-year-old overgrown openings before the hardwoods are suppressed.

For months or years between the cutting and site preparation the land is a gnarled mess of severed trunks and limbs, tangled undergrowth struggling to revive, and cull trees (rejected from the harvest because of defects or smallness) standing with broken tops, limbs, and bark. The openings where loggers skidded and piled logs are compacted and barren, until weeds appear. Few animals venture in. Humans stay out unless seeking firewood.

A year or more after site preparation (bulldozing, poisoning, and/or burning), when the vines and thorny plants enter in full force — Devil's club in the Northwest, catbriar and blackberry in the East and South — a human cannot enter without a machete. For the next several years, the commercial saplings and competing shrubbery, tangled with vines and briars, continue to impede passage. When the clones become pole trees, they form a dense stand, shading out most of the undergrowth. Very few animals choose to enter.

See Color Plate 4.

About this time, in most places, thinners bulldoze, saw, girdle, or poison some of the trees. If it is a pre-commercial thinning, they leave poles all over the ground. Even during commercial thinning, when they remove poles, they leave the same kind. Few species of shrubs, forbs, or animals remain.

After decades of thinnings — forty to fifty years in the South, longer elsewhere — trees will be better spaced, and larger, but almost all of one kind. No people will visit the stand. Soon the loggers again clearcut the stand, and the cycle resumes.

In some regions, managers (especially if they plant legumes) can raise White-tailed deer in clearcuts, but even so, a forest of clearcuts is not natural habitat; and for many hunters, an important part of the hunt is to return to nature.

Overall, clearcutting an area eliminates its recreational opportunities.

CLEARCUTTING COMPACTS AND ERODES THE SOIL, DEMOLISHING THE BASIS OF LIFE

Clearcutting shatters the delicate balance of ions, air, water, chemicals, and organisms in the soil and leaf litter that comprise the building blocks of all life. This balance does not restore itself completely for thousands of years, if ever. Robert R. Curry, geologist, of the University of Montana, testimony before the House Agriculture Committee, 1974.

When they log all the commercial trees in one or two operations, they force out much of the sub-surface air that is vital to most organisms that enrich the soil. They also expose the soil to erosion, and to the leaching out of nutrients by rain.

When they clear or kill the remaining vegetation to make way for commercial trees, they increase these losses drastically.

A 1983 study by Blackburn, et al, of Texas A&M University, reported that after tracts were clearcut, and the residual trees, shrubs, and other plants were pushed into windrows by dozers with brush rakes (as is generally done in Forest Service operations in the South), the sediment losses in the first year were nine times as large as in undisturbed control tracts. The clearcutting in that study was conducted more carefully than Forest Service clearcuts. Uncut buffers were left along stream courses, and no logs were skidded across small streams. The Forest Service has employed Dr. Blackburn full time.

Moreover, the clearcuts in the study were relatively small, only 6.37 to 6.78 acres each. Forest Service clearcuts average twenty to thirty acres. Erosion increases exponentially with the largeness of the clearcut. (Gordon Robinson, 1977). After a fourteen-acre clearcut, the sediment loss would be more than eighty-one times that in an uncut tract. The loss on a thirty-acre tract is inconceivable. Also, the clearcuts in the Texas study were on slopes of four to twenty-five degrees, very little of the latter. On steeper slopes, the losses would increase drastically. Studies in Utah, Illinois, North Carolina, California, (Dr. Robert R. Curry) and other regions show that clearcutting has resulted in large soil losses.

CLEARCUTTING SAPS THE SOIL OF NUTRIENTS

The Texas study reported that nitrate losses in the clearcut plots were 34 times the losses in the undisturbed plots. Losses of other nutrients included ammonia, 2 times; Ortho-phosphorous, 4.5 times; total phosphorous, 23 times; potassium, 2 times; and magnesium, 1.5 times.

Studies in California, West Virginia and Georgia also showed far greater nutrient losses from clearcuts than from undisturbed plots.

As a result of nutrient losses, it is likely that even commercially pampered species will not grow as rapidly after a second and third clearcut as they did before the first clearcut. The tree exploiters will have to spend a lot of money on fertilizer. Even fertilizer will not supply essential trace elements lost in clearcutting.

Studies of sediment and nutrient loss often indicate a decrease in losses from the clearcuts after a year or two. However, as Robert R. Curry, said to the House Agriculture Committee in testimony on the National Forest Timber Reform Act of 1976:

> "When a forest is cut and a major component of its biologically-available nutrients are lost or removed through upset of biogeo-chemical pathways, some of the nutrient capital in these intermediate storage sites replaces that which was lost. Some researchers have said that this proves that weathering goes on rapidly and that apparent nutrient depletion demonstrated at numerous experimental forest sites is thus not a serious long-term problem. Others, however, point out that these intermediate storage sites are providing those nutrients and that they too can be depleted. This means that a forest can 'bounce back' to near full potential if seriously disturbed by some management practices for one or more times, but that ultimately repeatead mismanagement will set the biogeochemical treasury to zero and further capital accumulation will have to be determined by geologic primary weathering processes of many millennia."

That the soil losses are permanent was further attested by Dr. Curry as follows:

> "Even in the semi-arid low-productivity forests of Montana, we have documented accelerated nutrient losses following clear-cutting, and the losses of soil by physical erosion are being documented very widely. For example, the U.S. Forest Service has shown, on the Six Rivers National Forest in California, that no matter what management practices are applied, including the option of no activity, the erosion rates on the Fox Planning Unit will be on the order of 2 to 2.5 times presumed natural background rates for all the foreseeable future just because a portion of the unit has been cut and roaded in the past. In other words, recovery is never anticipated even with reforestation and road removal because, as well demonstrated by the U.S. Geological Survey in the watershed of Redwood National Park, the watersheds are disequilibrated and cannot recover no matter what man's efforts, within a great many human generations. This means that site conditions and soil productivity will continue to decline through soil erosion because the balance between rainfall, infiltration, runoff, stream sedimentation and bank undercutting has been upset."

CLEARCUTTING INCREASES RAIN RUN-OFF, LOWERS GROUND WATER TABLE

In an undisturbed forest, trees and other vegetation break the force of rainfall, absorb some of it through their roots, and assist the soil in receiving, absorbing, and storing more of it. After clearcutting and site depredation the soil loses sponginess and ability to absorb and filter rainwater and snow melt.

In the Texas study, the runoff after clearcutting and shearing (bulldozing with a sharp blade so as to cut off vegetation at ground level) was more than five times as great as on undisturbed replicates. Virtually all studies show greater run-off after clearcutting, regardless of whether it is followed by site preparation.

In Colorado, and elsewhere in the Rockies, ingenious Forest Service personnel argued that increased runoff is an added economic benefit of clearcutting. They said that the extra runoff added valuable water to Colorado reservoirs. (Richard Domingue, *Forest Watch*, July 1986.) Opponents shot down this ludicrous claim by pointing out that the water is more valuable when stored in the soil and released gradually, rather than increasing the crests of floods in periods of high rainfall and snow melt, when there is a surplus of run-off anyhow.

Rain and snow-melt that filter into the ground provide essential sustenance for trees and other vegetation during dry periods. Also, by seeping out as perennial springs, such waters keep streams flowing constantly to the benefit of aquatic life.

CLEARCUTTING SCOURS, SILTS, AND POLLUTES STREAMS, RUINS FISHING

Heavy rains wash litter and hunks of mud from clearcuts into streams, scouring the banks, and deposit silt on stream bottoms. The resultant widening and flattening of streams decreases the depths of pools and rapids. Sediment covers pebbles that salmon and other species need for spawning and covers and kills fish eggs. Excessive litter chokes off runs of salmon and other migratory species. Stream fishermen have no sentiment for sediment.

See photo "Silt Proves Guilt."

Woody debris washed down from clearcuts changes the chemical and physical balance of streams and lakes. Even worse, pesticides are washed down from forests under even-age management,

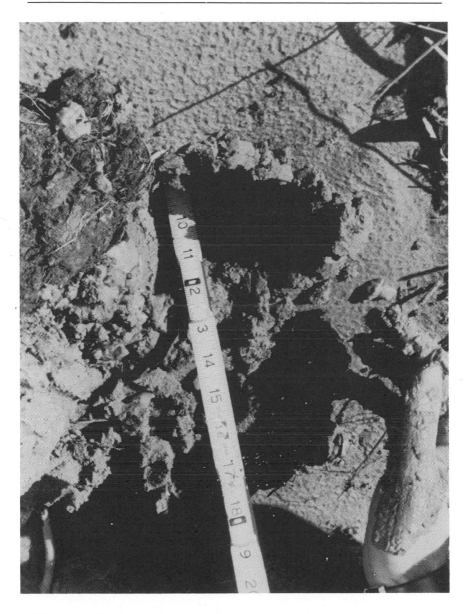

"Silt Proves Guilt," Sam Houston NF, Texas (Southeastern), 1979.
    The infamous Briar Creek clearcut, followed by a rain, deposited twelve inches of silt in the swollen creek (receded before this photo). This clearcut proceeded in an inventoried area in spite of Forest Service guidelines precluding any logging until congressional review of agency decision against wilderness designation.

and fertilizers will also be, as repeated clearcuts make their use necessary to regrow trees.

See photo "Mudballs for Swan Lake."

EVEN-AGE MEANS "ANTISEPTIC"

In several steps of even-age management, federal agencies are lavish in the use of biocides.

In site preparation after a clearcut, seed tree, or shelterwood cut, the Forest Service often injects Velpar or other herbicides into the trees by spear or hypohatchet.

See Color Plate 7.

The agency spreads Velpar, Triclopyr, or Hexazinon on the ground around less profitable hardwoods. These poisons kill not only standing trees but also all organisms in the soil where the poison is spread.

See Photo "Warning in the Ouachita."

Later, as new plants spring up in competition with the favored species even-age foresters often kill them by spreading or spraying herbicies. The Forest Service even sprays Roundup to kill native pine seedlings that spring up in competition with cloned "super-pines."

At any stage, even-age foresters are likely to use fungicides and other biocides to "control" various tree diseases.

They also use insecticides. The Forest Service Supervisor in Texas even proposed Methyl Bromide to destroy colonies of leaf-cutting ants, because these ants include pine seedlings among the plants that they strip. When citizens appealed, he withdrew his proposal.

In various parts of the country, the Forest Service has sprayed aerially to protect a commercial species from insects or from competition by other species.

All these poisons are tools of even-age man, to protect commercial trees from natural competition. They all can sicken vertebrates and humans.

MORE PINES BRING MORE BEETLES, LEADING TO MORE PINE PLANTATIONS AND MORE BEETLES

An elemental principle of ecology is that the denser is the population of a certain species, the more susceptible it is to insects and disease. This principle of density dependence became apparent

"Mudballs for Swan Lake," Flathead NF, Montana, 1988. By James R. Conner.
Now covered with nature's white sheets these clearcuts lie immediately above
Swan Lake, fouling a previously natural setting and causing periodic muddying of the
lake. The agency called the closest cut "Sweet Mary." The cut adjoining to its left is
a seed tree cut, with several seed trees per acre. These will be removed later.

"Warning in the Ouachita," Ouachita NF, Oklahoma, 1986.
    This legally required notice warns the reader that Velpar has been sprayed here in Beech Creek Unit, at that time inventoried as potential wilderness and, in 1988, protected by Congress from even-age management practices as part of the Winding Stair Mountain National Recreation Area and Indian Nations National Scenic and Wildlife Area.

during the 1983–1986 desecration of National Forests in Texas with a stated purpose of controlling the Southern pine beetle.

Throughout the Gulf Coastal Plain, the Forest Service has been suppressing hardwoods for fifty years in an effort to grow more pines. The resultant dense growth of pines led to the worst epidemic of Southern pine beetles in history.

In July 1983, the Forest Service in Texas attacked the beetles, pines, and wilderness proposals. It made thousands of pine timber sales in buffer zones around beetle spots. Hordes of beetles flew over the buffers and joined other hordes already scattered through the forests. The epidemic proceeded unabated, reaching a peak in 1985. Pine farmers have been cutting buffers around beetle spots for decades, without controlling epidemics, but this time, sadly, they cut thousands of acres in proposed wildernesses, and continued even after Congress designated five areas as wilderness.

See cartoon by Billy Hallmon.

Whenever they cut a buffer of pines, loggers knock the limbs and tops off most of the hardwood trees in the buffer zone. But the oaks, hickories, gums, and cherries come back on natural hardwood and hardwood/pine sites. These sites should have been allowed to return to native vegetation, but the Forest Service set out to bulldoze down all the hardwoods and to plant only pines.

In the Four Notch, a former wilderness planning area, the Forest Service contracted for a 105-ton tree crusher to knock down and crush all plants that remained on 2,600 acres where loggers had eliminated most of the pines by cutting beetle buffers. Earth First!ers chained themselves to trees and even to the tree crusher, to stop the devastation. This action and subsequent wet weather prevented the Forest Service from resuming tree crushing until spring of 1987.

The attorney-general of Texas sought an injunction under the National Environmental Policy Act. The U.S. District Court in Houston denied any relief.

Upon completing the crushing, the Forest Service followed through with a helitorch burn, preparatory to planting Loblolly pines. It looks like another great break-through by even-aged man. What will he do when the beetles again infest all of his pines?

See newspaper cartoon.

— Billy Hallmon

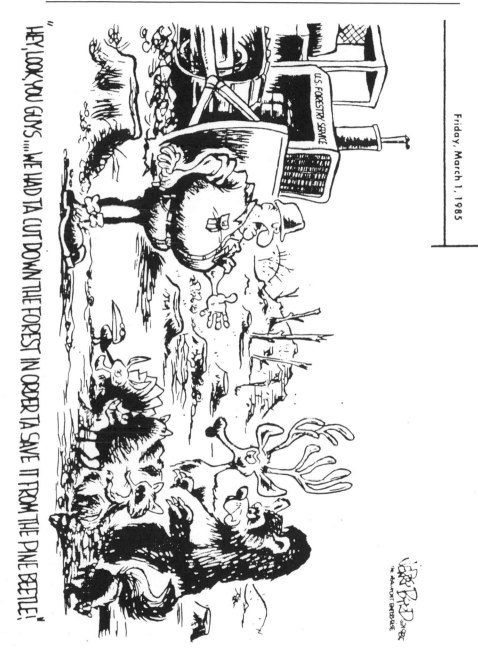

"HEY, LOOK YOU GUYS.... WE HAD TA CUT DOWN THE FOREST IN ORDER TA SAVE IT FROM THE PINE BEETLE!"

Friday, March 1, 1985

— Beaumont Enterprise

BLOWDOWNS AND BEACHHEADS

Clearcutting exposes surrounding trees to direct wind. Blowdowns are frequent on the edge of clearcuts. The Forest Service seizes upon blowdowns as excuses for "salvage" clearcuts. These cuts are not limited to damaged trees, but include many healthy trees around them. Examples include a 1986 "salvage" cut in the "Fly Area" on the North Fork of the Snoqualmie River in Wenatchee N.F., Washington, where the Forest Service sold Douglas-firs 180 feet tall in an old-growth grove which environmentalists had long been contesting with the Forest Service.

At the edge of a clearcut, the sun can cast sidelight into surrounding forests that are not naturally exposed to this intensity of light. Species of early succession then penetrate the old forest for distances of up to 180 feet, displacing some of the native species, and spawning beachheads of weeds.

WORSENS GLOBAL WARMING, OZONE DEPLETION

Clearcutting decreases the green biomass on earth. After logging, anyone can see the reduction. After site preparation, little or no green remains.

The chlorophyll-rich foliage is what controls carbon dioxide, storing the carbon in stems, trunks, and roots while releasing the oxygen into the atmosphere. Life depends on an adequacy of oxygen. Life, as we live it, also depends on holding the temperature within its present range. Unless curbed, the global warming trend (Greenhouse Effect) is likely to change the world in the next thirty to fifty years.

Roughly twenty-five percent of the increase in carbon dioxide on earth since humans started burning carbon-based fossil fuels is generally attributed to deforestation (the other seventy-five percent to fuel emissions).

An excess of carbon dioxide also contributes to reduction of the ozone layer in the stratosphere, exposing the skins of most animals to cancer-causing sun rays.

Humans are clearcutting all the way around the globe. The effect on global warming is probably heaviest in the tropics, because of denser biomass there. But the effect lasts longer in temperate zones, where the foliage takes longer to return to normal density.

Nobody has scientifically compared the losses of green biomass in different logging systems.

We already know that a clearcut reduces the green biomass nearly to zero for weeks in the tropics and almost a year in most of the United States. We also know that the foliage does not regain its former density for many years.

Selection logging somewhat reduces the foliage for less than a year. The uncut vegetation increases its foliage within days, in the growing season. Selection is clearly the superior silvicultural system for combatting global warming and ozone depletion.

Prescribed burning causes a reduction of foliage when used with either system of growing timber. Foresters use it more often with even-age. They use it least often in all-age all-species selection management, because foresters using that variation are least motivated to suppress hardwoods. A major purpose of prescribed burning in commercial pine stands is the suppression of hardwoods.

In the South, Pacific Northwest, and some other regions, foresters often raise commercial trees to a greater density at maturity under even-age than under selection, tending toward balancing out the huge superiority of foliage in selection during the first years after logging. The denser the commercial trees, the more susceptible they are to insects and diseases. The threat of bark beetles, alone, requires constraints upon the density of conifers in the South and West, so that even-age foresters can never fully catch up with succession management in average volume of green biomass per year.

After many studies, scientists may agree that the effect of clearcutting in the United States on global warming and ozone depletion is relatively small. Yet each small fraction joins with the rest to achieve a devastating cumulative effect. The whole carbon dioxide problem is so widespread that we must attack it everywhere we can. Our very survival is in jeopardy.

The consequences are so deadly that every human should share in the responsibility to maintain his/her local vegetation as close as possible to its natural level. Therefore, we must bring clearcutting to an end, everywhere, as a silvicultural system.

PRESCRIBED (CONTRIVED) BURNING, ANOTHER WEAPON AGAINST NATIVE DIVERSITY

The most often-used gene-ocidal weapon of Forest Service people in the South is prescribed burning. They burn pine stands repeatedly to keep other vegetation from attaining heights above ten or fifteen feet. The main victims are hardwood trees, the bark of which cannot resist fire the way pine bark can. The usual interval between prescribed burns is two to five years. The burners claim to be mimicking the frequency of wildfires (lightning fires) before humans built roads and other firebreaks, and began fire-fighting. Actually, they have no proof of what the fire frequency was in nature. They could find out by careful dendrochronology, and, in some areas, palynology, but they don't want to know the truth because it might shatter their excuse for burning.

In a study of a protected Longleaf pine stand in East Texas with trees up to eighty years of age, dendrologists found evidence of only two burns. Longleaf pine is considered to be a fire-climax or fire-sub-climax species. Natural fires are vital to their maintaining optimum density. But the Forest Service is burning Longleaf stands every two to five years.

Prescribe-burn advocates argue that fires as small as prescribed burns do not leave detectable scars, so dendrologists cannot establish the full fire frequency before human influence. When scientists are uncertain, we should not burn. The burden of proof is upon those who wish to manipulate.

Even in wet Southeast Alaska, where natural fires are insignificant, a Forest Service District Ranger in Tongass N.F. is striving to set a precedent for prescribed burning. He wants to burn a Sitka spruce stand near Tenakee Springs for "wildlife" purposes. In many eastern forests, the Service burns frequently "for white-tail deer." Generally, the real purpose is to suppress hardwoods.

An effect of burning a site more often than is natural is to favor fire-adapted species over native species. An unnatural fire regime changes the relative density of plant species and eliminates some species altogether, with a similar effect on animals associated with those plants. A host of plants and animals, mostly small ones, are dependent upon the leaf-litter on the forest floor. Prescribed burns, far more than natural fires, destroy the leaf litter, and therefore many species. *Timber Management Is Not Wildlife Management*, Steven P. Christman, 4th Ann. Mtg., Gopher Tortoise Council, pp. 5–18, 1983.

Burning at a different season than that of lightning fires similarly disrupts natural communities. In the South, the Forest Service prefers to burn in winter, for effectiveness in suppressing hardwoods and for controllability. A recent Florida study shows that burning in winter results in different plant compositions from those that prevail under a lightning fire (late summer) regime. (Mary M. Davis, *The Effect of Season of Fire upon Flowering of Forbs in Longleaf Pine-Wiregrass Forests,* Florida State University, 1985.)

In a seminar at Stephen F. Austin State University, May 20, 1987, Robert M. Farrar, of the Southern Forest Experiment Station, stated that prescribed burning has been overly frequent.

In brief, contrived burners are impairing our natural heritage in order to raise more lumber for sale.

AS CLEARCUTS MULTIPLY,
THEIR EFFECTS SKYROCKET

So far, we've discussed the disastrous effects of individual clearcuts. Now, we want to explain how these effects increase exponentially as clearcuts spread like cancer over most of a forest.

As clearcuts connect up with each other, erosion increases exponentially; and due to fragmentation, the uncut remnants, as well as the clearcuts, lose their native diversity.

See photos "Clearcutting on a Rampage" and "Clobbered."

Even when clearcuts are still separated by uncut stands, the latter cannot retain their full diversity, because the clearcutting has made them mere fragments of the original forest. The smaller a natural area is, the fewer species can survive there.

When clearcutting becomes pervasive, even wildlife that can survive in a partly clearcut forest, (white-tailed deer) decline in vigor from inadequate diet and shelter, especially in cold winters. In stressful conditions, big die-offs occur. All wandering animals are subjected to the ever-increasing effects of herbicides and pesticides. Furthermore, because run-off of sediment particles increases in speed and quantity as rain washes downhill, they scour the particles soil in large clearings more severely than in small. As clearings merge, run-off continues ever faster from one clearing to the next, even where growth has sprung up in older clearcuts. Therefore, a downhill clearcut suffers more than one uphill from it.

The run-off silts up entire streams. Soil nutrients plummet at the same increased rate. The clearcutting surrounds and makes oases of wildernesses, causing blowdowns and weed invasions even there.

Recreationists can no longer get away from the sights and sounds of cutting except in wildernesses.

In toto, as clearcuts become more pervasive, their ravages increase at an even greater rate.

Clearcutters can argue that a single clearcut is needed in a certain place for a certain reason. An example they give is where a wildfire burned down a low-rainfall forest decades ago, and the trees that survived are stunted and the rest of the area is overgrown with shrubs that prevent the regeneration of commercial trees.

Even if that condition prevailed in a given stand, it would not justify the clearcutting, bit by bit, of almost an entire forest.

We must not let anyone divert our clearcutting fight into a series of contests over individual stands. Our case against wholesale clearcutting is infinitely stronger — invincible.

Arguing over a single clearcut while ignoring the extent of wholesale clearcutting would be like criticizing a single drink without regard to the harmful effects of over-drinking.

This is not to say that we should not use flagrant individual clearcuts as examples, to demonstrate our point. It is to say that we should focus on the big picture — wholesale, massive, indiscriminate commercial tree farming.

THEY ARE CLEARCUTTING
ALMOST ALL AVAILABLE TIMBER

We might have less cause for alarm about the clearcutting of federal timberlands if the remainder were under better management. There might be plenty of forests where state and private owners would preserve native diversity, wildlife could flourish, and the burgeoning populations of humans could enjoy deep woods free of radical surgery.

Unfortunately, not only federal lands are being clearcut. States with timberlands are selling the timber for clearcuts, and most timber companies have their lands under even-age management at even lower rotation periods (20 to 80 years) than the federal agencies (70 to 120 years).

In brief, almost all the available timberland in the United States will be clearcut, unless citizens arise and curtail it.

OLD GROWTH: THE JEWELS IN THE MATRIX

Fortunately, Congress and state legislatures have protected some parcels of native diversity from any logging whatsoever. These preserves are mainly national parks and wildernesses, comprising 130 million acres, a substantial part of which are forested. Only about three million more acres of forest remain that have never been logged, mainly in the Pacific Northwest. They contain priceless ecosystems. Congress should preserve every acre of them.

But even where protected from logging, these relatively small remnants of old growth will be vulnerable to internal attrition if we let our federal agencies continue to clearcut around them. Our ancient forests will be like jewels that corrode without a matrix, isolated from other forests and from the flow of plant and animal life that enables natural areas to survive and to evolve through the changes that this planet experiences, even without the influence of human beings.

The further that clearcutting takes place in the federal forests the closer our remaining ancient forests approach the condition of biogeographical islands, life systems that lose species and texture as a result of physical and genetic isolation.

Under the present trend, even though we have seemingly vast preserves such as Yellowstone, we are losing the Grizzly bear, Timber wolf, Wolverine, Spotted owl, Red-cockaded woodpecker, and numerous other forest species, great and small. To save our natural species and ecosystems, we need to deal not only with the jewels, but also with the matrices in which they stay in place.

We should prevail upon Congress to give every potential area the superior protection of wilderness designation, and short of that, should influence the Forest Service to save old-growth stands in a special category. Between such preserves, in the vast interconnecting acreages that will remain as "available commercial timberland," we citizens must clamp down on clearcutting. To achieve this end, our best hope is the United States Congress.

PART III

The Vastly Superior Alternative

INDIVIDUAL-TREE SELECTION IS THE WAY TO GROW

The only environmentally sound timber management system is individual-tree selection, in which foresters mark for cutting the most mature trees and the ones to be thinned or culled, so that most of the stand will live on to produce more seedlings and to grow more quality timber. This is the classic method. The Forest Service calls the system uneven-age or all-age management because each stand has trees of several ages.

See Color Plates 17–25.

I have visited selection systems, large and small, in West Germany, England, and nine states, and I say without reservation that they all conserve far more leaf-litter, wildlife, and native diversity than any form of clearcutting. Environmentally, there is no comparison between the two. Leaf litter is vital to a host of species in the base of the food chain, says wildlife biologist, Dr. Steven P. Christman, of Florida University.

In every selection forest, at least two-thirds of the area is in the shade of tall trees. There is a sub-canopy of partly grown trees, generally of various ages. At a still lower level, saplings are coming on, and shrubs and wildflowers of many species.

Wilmon Timberlands manages 50,000 acres under the selection system in southwestern Alabama. There, I saw such stands in many forest types — Nuttall oak/Pignut hickory/Tulip poplar; White oak/Loblolly pine/Black gum; Shortleaf pine/Southern red oak/White ash/ and Longleaf pine/Bluejack oak. Azaleas and Mountain laurel and a host of other wildflowers were blooming. The streams were clear. Numerous species of birds were singing. Deer leaped ahead of us at many points. Some stands were on low and wet ground. Others were high and steep. All were beautiful, even where they had recently harvested. And at Wilmon, they seldom have to burn or use chemicals.

A Forest Service team visited Wilmon Timberlands, about three years ago, but they do not acknowledge the existence of Wilmon in any of their environmental impact statements.

WHY DO THE BUREAUCRATS AVOID INDIVIDUAL TREE SELECTION?

In answer to this big question, let us first analyze three reasons that they give.

1. They Say They Have to Clearcut to Grow Their Chosen Species.

The Forest Service insists that the various pines and hardwoods that bring the best market returns are too shade-intolerant to regenerate in the selection system. They say that, without radical clearing, Loblolly pines in the Gulf Coastal Plain, Nuttall oaks in moist sites of the Deep South, Black cherry on some Appalachian Mountain sites, Ponderosa and Sugar pine in the Rockies, Lodgepole pine further west, and Douglas-fir on the West Coast, cannot get started as seedlings and saplings in adequate numbers to grow into well-stocked stands.

Selection foresters prove this to be false. Over and over, they have demonstrated excellent natural regeneration in individual-tree selection forests. Gordon Robinson did it with Douglas-fir and Ponderosa pine on a million acres of Southern Pacific Transportation Company lands in California and Oregon. Individual Tree Selection Management does it in Oregon. Leo Drey regenerates Southern Red oak, White oak and Shortleaf pine on 173,000 acres in Missouri. Chuck Stoddard regenerates Red pine and other species naturally in Wisconsin. Leon Tolliver does it with Northern red oak and Tulip poplar on his week-end 400 acres near Bedford, Indiana. Leon Neel regenerates Longleaf pine and various hardwoods that way in Southern Georgia and Frank Stewart, Jr. regenerates a wide diversity on varying sites in Alabama. Hundreds of others raise many forest types productively on many kinds of sites.

I have observed the tiny sprouts coming up by the hundreds around my feet in most of these forests. It can be done. It is being done on millions of acres.

Even some Forest Service experts say that you can successfully regenerate Loblolly and Shortleaf pines under the individual-tree selection method. They are doing it at Crossett Experimental Forest, Southern Forest Experimental Station, Monticello, Arkansas, Bulletin 872, June 1984, Division of Agriculture, University of Arkansas, Fayetteville.

2. They Say Selection Harvesting Is a Lost Art.

The Forest Service argues that a timber owner can no longer find foresters who know how and when to select the trees that should be removed and chain-saw operators who can fell trees without excessively damaging the "save" trees.

The timber industry makes grants to forestry schools, including research grants and chair endowments. Schools that depend most heavily on timber industry grants tend to emphasize even-age management. This does create a growing shortage of all-around foresters. Nevertheless, you can still find some in every region and selective harvesting skills will revive rapidly if we curtail clearcutting.

As to operators, numerous loggers in every region can still aim the drop so that the unharvested trees in a selection stand are not damaged. They do so for the landowners who selectively harvest. They also aim the drop when thinning even-age stands.

When he went into the selection system, Paul Shaffner, of Fordyce, Arkansas, had to train his chain-saw contractors how to fell marked trees more cleanly. The initial training cost him some dollars, but he soon made up for it in increased vigor of the trees saved.

Shaffner obtained his forestry degree at Yale University, where they still teach selection management, as well as clearcutting.

3. They Say That Selection Management Requires More Roads Than Even-Age.

In the Monongahela National Forest Plan and EIS (July 1986), the Forest Service wooed some citizen groups away from a selection alternative by claiming that selection required more roads. Agency planners pulled this trick by arbitrarily allowing more public use of the roads in the selection than the even-age alternative, and by claiming that uneven-age requires more frequent entries (although this system requires no site preparation, and no burning, and no thinning other than at regular harvest time). The EIS ignored the fact that selection forestry can be practiced all the way to the edge of existing roads where clearcutting is not allowed for aesthetic reasons.

In actual practice, selection forests require no greater road mileage nor higher standards than even-age management. In fact, the roads that I saw on selection forests were narrower than most Forest Service roads, and were often closed canopy, yet quite passable in all seasons.

See Color Plates 21 and 25.

I have observed numerous wash-outs on Forest Service roads.

In the Texas Plan (May 1987), the Forest Service attempted to discredit selection management by saying, again, that selection management requires more frequent use and maintenance of roads. This time, they claimed that the extra maintenance caused more erosion. They actually had the gall to boast less erosion from even-age than from selection management!

4. They Say Clearcutting Brings Bigger Dollars.

When you argue with clearcutters down to the bottom line, their main reason for insisting on clearcutting becomes just that, the bottom line.

In the 1976 Texas clearcutting case under the Monongahela case precedent of 1974, Forest Service and timber company witnesses testified that selective harvesting was not profitable. They swore that nobody could stay in business doing it. The environmentalists found Paul Shaffner, a timber operator from Arkansas, who took the stand against the Forest Service and proved that he was making a satisfactory profit at selection harvesting. Obviously, he was not buying any timber from the Forest Service.

Many Texas timber owners are making a profit on individual-tree selection stands.

Louisiana Pacific's Southern Division practices individual-tree selection on its own lands and many other lands throughout the South that it manages for smaller owners.

Here is a passage from LP's 1987 slick-paper color brochure:

"Louisiana-Pacific's motto, 'Helping the forest work for people,' starts with LP Forestry's environmentally sound forest management policy of single tree selection, which allows the forest to grow and reproduce naturally. The excessive costs and detrimental environmental impacts associated with clear-cutting are avoided."

When the Forest Service offers a clearcut sale, it gives no choice to LP or anyone else to use selection harvesting. So LP-Southern clearcuts on Forest Service land, a genuine tragedy.

Temple-Eastex, Inc., largest timber owner in Texas, used selective harvesting until it merged with Time, Inc. Arthur Temple, who then headed the combined company, told me that the financial experts in New York showed him figures indicating that clearcutting was more profitable, so he permitted the change to clearcutting. Even after spinning back to a separate company, the Temple company continued to clearcut, although some of its stands along the highway are still featured by old "Perpetual Forest" signs.

See photo "Their Showcase Is Selection."

5. They Don't Tell You How Expensive Clearcutting Is.

The Forest Service does not acknowledge the biggest expense of clearcutting — interest charges. They invest a lot of money for site preparation and planting and do not receive most of their returns until the timber sale some 40 to 120 years later. This involves a heavy charge for the use of money, realistically at least 7.5%, cumulative. The Forest Service should include that interest in its sale price to the company that buys the timber. But the Service uses a much lower figure, four percent. On some items, it omits the interest cost altogether.

When we apply a realistic interest rate (under sound economic procedures reversed into a "discount" rate), the costs of clearcutting exceed the returns in almost all national forests, according to forest economist Randal O'Toole in Citizen's Guide to Forestry and Economics.

Selection harvesting is different. It does not involve site preparation and planting (a major saving in itself). It involves a harvest every five to twenty years. Pre-commercial thinning is done at the same time, reducing that cost. Once sustained yield is established in a stand, the expenses forever after are mostly in the same year as the harvest, and altogether in the same decade or so. The interest charges are minimal.

Regardless of using a low discount rate and taking certain

"Their Showcase is Selection," Angelina National Forest 1988.
    Although this timber company has gone over to even-age management, it contin-ues selection on about eight stands along highways, and is rightfully proud of it.

other advantages, the Forest Service Forplan (computerized) run of March 1986, for El Dorado National Forest in the California Sierras, indicated a relatively small difference in net present value between individual tree selection ($1.64 billion) and even-age management ($1.87 billion). The Forest Service generally uses net present value in its forest plans.

Dr. James B. Baker, director of the Forest Service Experiment Station at Monticello, Arkansas, compared the economics of selection and even-age over a fifty-year period. He reported a cost efficiency of "conventional" selection at 143.2 board feet of sawlogs produced per dollar of costs, compared to 55.2 for an even-aged plantation, a $2^1/2$ to 1 advantage. Adding pulp and poles to the picture, the advantage decreased to about 20%. But our national forests are mainly in the sawlog business.

Using a discount rate of 7%, Baker also calculated net present value at 341 for selection and 444 for plantation, but he later wrote:

> "The high NPV for even-aged plantation management is misleading in that it resulted more from the relatively large investment required by the system than from its efficiency. The results of this comparison indicate that a landowner should select this system only if he desires one of the noneconomic benefits associated with it — such as maximum total output or production, the opportunity to plant superior seedlings, or ease of management."

In a commentary on the Baker paper, Texas forester Bill Carroll wrote:

> "Under the multiple use and other concepts in our national forests, 'maximum total output,' 'superior seedlings' and 'ease of management' should give way to public benefit. Furthermore, the Forest Service's use of 'superior seedlings' on a grand scale is reducing our native diversity and is saddling our timber stock with strains that are more susceptible to insects and diseases."

A private company might be able to justify to its stockholders the use of drastic surgery on its lands in order to produce a larger profit. To damage the public lands for such a slender increase in returns is unconscionable. The government is not supposed to be driven by the profit motive in running the public lands, especially not at the expense of native diversity, wildlife, recreation, soil, and other benefits to present and future generations. Of course, the

Forest Service says it has all those other benefits in mind as well as profits, but that answer is contrived, as we shall discuss.

In many regions, there is probably some labor saving in the logging stage of clearcutting because, with larger openings and with operators intending to knock down all the vegetation anyhow, loggers can use heavier skidders and can operate them at a higher speed. The Forest Service claims that intensive logging, even during market slumps, is necessary to provide employment. If that is true, then the selection system would be preferable, since it requires more employees.

Furthermore, the Forest Service is in no position to insist on maximum profits from its sales. It sells its timber in all but two regions at a loss to the American taxpayer. When there is a market glut and offerings fail to attract bidders, the Forest Service re-offers its timber at lower minimum prices, suffering even greater losses.

Since raising most species of trees is something the Forest Service cannot do under even-age management without selling below cost, there is no sense in ripping up our national forests under this method. We would do better to let private timberlands supply that portion of our timber demand.

In short, the Forest Service's economic defense of even-age management is skewed.

6. They Don't Count The Intangible Losses.

The Forest Service does not take into account many of the costs of cutting timber that make timber harvesting in the national forests even more of a waste of money than economists indicate. Among these costs are losses of soil, water quality, wildlife habitat, native diversity, and natural open space recreation. They are left out of benefit/cost analyses because they are not readily quantified.

Although the Forest Service refuses to assign dollars to decreases in acreages for wildlife and recreation. John White, assistant director of the Forest Service in Washington, in an interview with the *Knoxville News-Sentinel* published May 10, 1987, showed how the Forest Service takes advantage of wildlife and recreation benefits. Admitting that "some" national forests lose money on timber sales, White added that some timber sales are designed to achieve some wildlife objective, and concluded ". . . we do receive some benefits in wildlife protection, as well as some recreational uses."

In Monongahela National Forest, staffers showed us several clearcuts that they had the nerve to claim were designed for Black bear and Varying hare (Snowshoe rabbit), although there were already numerous other clearcuts available for whatever tendencies Black bear might have to leave the deep forests to which they are well adapted, and for Varying hare, as well.

The Forest Service also fails to include the cost of fertilizers that would be necessary because of zooming losses of soil nutrients resulting from repeated clearcuts.

7. They Claim that Selection Cannot Be Done on a Grand Scale.

In its recent forest plans, the Forest Service has included an ever-evolving appendix delineating the arguments against selection management. Always adept at defenses, the bureaucrats claim that the selection system is too complex, variable, and tree-specific to fill the need for forest-wide production predictions and planning ("forest-level timber regulation," they call it). They say that stable annual production is necessary for a big agency and the economy that it serves.

The bureaucrats fail to note that several private companies are successfully regulating timber under the selection system on acreages comparable to national forests. These include Louisiana-Pacific, on one million acres in the South, Leo Drey on 153,000 acres in Missouri, and Collins Pine on 87,000 acres in California. The Forest Service, itself, successfully managed to inventory and to regulate the national forest timber on the selection basis until 1964, when it switched to clearcutting.

Although requiring greater knowledge of the forest and skill in implementation, selection management allows more accurate growth predictions than even-age, because under selection, predictions are based more sensitively on what is happening in the forest down to the individual trees in inventory plots.

SELECTION IS NOT FOOL-PROOF

Individual-tree selection is not fool-proof, or distortion-proof. The Forest Service's Southern Forest Experiment Station near Crossett, Arkansas, employs this method to raise mixed pulpwood on some stands, and only pine sawlogs on other stands. Unlike at Wilmon Timberlands, the Forest Service at Ashley County uses chemicals heavily to suppress hardwoods. If Congress curtails clearcutting on federal lands, the bureaucracies might continue to desecrate native diversity by practicing uneven-age management of a single commercial species, suppressing all competitive trees and shrubs. Other species would also suffer. In such stands, the native ecosystems disappear.

To avert any such evasion, the law must not only restrain clearcutting but also require preservation of native diversity.

HOW THEY BURIED SELECTION MANAGEMENT

Until the National Forest Management Act of 1976 (NFMA), selection harvesting was the only legal cutting system for the Forest Service. Nevertheless, in 1964 the agency began widespread clear-cutting. In 1974, in the famous Monongahela case by the Natural Resources Defense Council, the U.S. Court of Appeals in the Fourth District, including West Virginia, blocked further clearcutting in that district. Elsewhere, the bureaucracy continued clearcutting full blast.

In 1976, a federal District Court temporarily enjoined the Forest Service from further clearcutting in Texas (see *Sterile Forest*). Later that year, at the prodding of the Forest Service and some major timber interests and heavy equipment sellers that were entrenched in clearcutting, Congress passed NFMA, repealing the old law against clearcutting.

Since then, it has been even-age management all the way.

HOW THEY DISTORTED GROUP SELECTION

Some foresters who wanted to avoid the evils of even-age management, and yet to grow species like Tulip-poplar that need substantial sunlight, invented group selection, the raising and harvesting of commercial trees in multi-age units of less than 1/10 acre. This method is like individual-tree selection, except two or more trees are marked and harvested alongside or near each other, to create a larger than one-tree opening. Some foresters classify it under selection management if the openings are less than 1/2 acre.

In several national forests, the new plans under NFMA provide for tiny fractions of the cutting to be "group selection," but as practiced by the Forest Service, this simply means small clearcuts from one to five acres, cleared and regenerated in one age group.

The Forest Service uses "group selection" as a device for claiming that it is willing to bend. Actually, its bend is scarcely more visible than that of a steel girder.

The new plans for the White Mountain National Forest in New Hampshire and the Green Mountain National Forest in Vermont are exceptions. In the White Mountain, clearcutting is down to thirty percent of the available commercial timber. The rest is selection, of sorts.

The Green Mountain plan is more complicated. For the first decade, "intensive uneven-age management" (group selection) is seventeen percent. "Intensive even-age" (mainly shelterwood) is forty percent. "Longer even-age" (120-year rotation) is forty-three percent. Local citizen groups have accepted both of these plans.

See photo "Group Selection."

In the Jefferson National Forest (Virginia), the Forest Service has agreed to follow Dr. Leon Minckler's advice in managing a five-acre group selection pilot project. Minckler, author of Woodland Ecology, 1985, is a former Forest Service researcher who has sharply criticized even-age management. The new Jefferson forest plan provides for up to 30,000 acres (out of one million in the forest) to be assigned to group selection.

Colorado and New Mexico plans allow small fractions of the cuts to be "group selection."

In the George Washington National Forest, (Virginia) only two hours southwest of Washington, D.C. the final plan allows the possibility of some individual-tree selection. The plan "identifies" 60,000 acres where uneven-age management may be practiced at some point in the plan's life. If the supervisor decides to practice individual selection on some or all of the acres, and the Chief lets him do it, that will still be only a small fraction of the million acres in that forest.

THE LEGISLATIVE PROBLEM
WITH GROUP SELECTION

Under a responsible silviculturist on a private forest, if no site preparation were allowed, group selection would not be as bad as clearcutting. But the Forest Service would probably use group selection to create openings large enough to plant commercial clones. There is no enforceable way to require agencies to limit group selection to widely scattered stands. On public lands, agencies could

"Group Selection," Jefferson National Forest 1987.

Dr. Leon S. Minckler, of Blacksburg, Virginia, former Forest Service researcher, has persuaded the Ranger to let him advise on the management of a group selection stand. Here it is after the first cutting. The soil and leaf litter are far less disturbed than in a clearcut. Natural regeneration is beginning.

eventually cut these tiny openings into back-to-back patch-clear-cuts throughout the forest, clearing as much as now, only in smaller bites. It would be like getting chewed up by piranhas instead of sharks.

Even if there were a way to restrict such cuts to one-half acre, the Forest Service would probably make them into even-age patches.

The only way to stop the Forest Service from finding a loop-hole in the law is to keep the law clear. Group selection is not susceptible to legal clarity.

PART IV

Answering the Timber Beasts

WHY DO BUREAUCRATS REALLY INSIST ON CLEARCUTTING?

1. Hierarchy means higher budgets.

Factors that goad the Forest Service to clearcut heavily are the strange laws that automatically increase their budget for doing so. They call them the Brush Disposal Act (1915) and the Knutson-Vandenberg Act (1930). They channel part of the purchaser's payments on a timber sale contract into a Forest Service account to pay anticipated costs for brush disposal, reforestation, roads, administration, and other expenses. The higher its cost estimates are, the more the Forest Service receives for its own budget, by-passing the rest of the government.

Brush disposal and reforestation include site preparation and planting. Selection harvesting does not involve those costs, so if the Forest Service used selection, less money would flow into its tills. Theoretically, a seed tree cut or shelterwood type of cut would involve natural regeneration, without site preparation, but the Forest Service tends to employ site preparation with such cuts so that it can get back more money.

In short, by insisting on even-age management, the Forest Service increases its budget. Increasing its budget is the objective of

53

a bureaucracy. Report No. 124, National Center for Policy Analysis, 1986.

The Brush Disposal Act and K-V serve as incentives for clearcutting, and also would serve as inducements for heavier cutting, even under selection management. Randal O'Toole, forest economist, in "Reforming the Forest Service," suggests that repealing Knutson-Vandenberg would constitute a major step toward improving Forest Service practices.

To understand the motivation of the Forest Service you have to look at the top of the Forest Service hierarchy. Just as in the case of the national harvesting quota, the Chief and his staff of loyal bureaucrats determine the clearcutting policy. Under the Resources Planning and Management Act, the regional foresters have made even-age the management system for entire regions. The individual forests have to follow that policy.

In some places, citizens are vocal and political enough to influence a forest supervisor toward a recommendation of selection. Even then, the supervisor has to go up through the regional forester. If any staff person presses for a large percentage of selection, he will run into a hierarchical defense of clearcutting and higher budgets. He who threatens higher budgets does not get promoted.

No matter how conscientious the average lower-level staffers of the Forest Service are, they will remain lower level if they don't play ball for higher budgets.

All things considered, Knutson-Vandenberg exerts an insidious influence in favor of clearcutting. However, it would take more than repeal of K-V to wrench the Forest Service out of the clearcutting trough.

2. Clearcutting fits well into tie-in timber sales.

In this practice, the Forest Service combines a sale of high quality timber with a cut that separately would lose money for the buyer. The combination gives the Forest Service a greater payment than would otherwise be obtainable, even though losing money on the sale of those stands that should not be cut. Report No. 124, NCPA, 1986.

3. The Chief and the Timber Barons.

Besides expanding its budget, another main objective of a bureaucracy is to protect its public image. Report No. 124, NCPA, supra. The organized timber interests who bid on clearcut sales and the newspapers in areas where timber is powerful support the FS to the hilt in its clearcutting appetite.

On the other hand, selection foresters are not well organized, and keep out of the clearcutting controversy.

4. Heavy equipment and heavy influence.

Also, clearcutting gives a special advantage to heavy equipment manufacturers, sellers, and owners. The timber companies that buy from the Forest Service own the heavy equipment required for clearcutting, or hire contractors who do. If you don't have access to such equipment, you cannot successfully compete for Forest Service clearcut sales. The heavier equipment makers, sellers, and owners have reason to keep the government in the clearcutting business and to support congresspersons who agree.

5. The computer connection.

Clearcutting is easier to mass-produce. The foresters can feed stand numbers into computers by age and site index, and can determine in the office when to sell how much. They can use all this data in the required forest plans. They do not have to know as much about individual tree growth. They do not need to go out in the hot sun or cold wind as often. They can sit around the air-conditioned office and think up arguments like the one in the new Texas plan — that even-age management is the only one that fits in with "forest-level timber regulation." As for selection harvesting, the Plan says, "No consideration is given to the relationship of one stand to the other." That is not true among the larger selection managers. They do forest-level management quite successfully.

6. The bureaucracy has inertia.

Now that it has set up wholesale clearcutting, it resists change.

These are the real reasons that the Forest Service will bend truths in order to stick with clearcutting. In a later section we will discuss the reasons that they have devised.

IF THEY CANNOT MANAGE A STAND ON A SELECTION BASIS THEY SHOULD NOT CUT IT AT ALL

There may be no way that the Forest Service can produce Lodgepole pine economically. The same applies to Douglas-fir, except in Western Oregon and Washington. In some regions, even with Ponderosa pine, the government can avoid a loss only under low intensity forestry. This means no hand planting, herbicides, spraying of fertilizers, or pre-commercial thinnings. The selection system is low intensity forestry.

Forest economist Randal O'Toole states in *The Citizens Guide to Forestry and Economics:* "Heavy investments in second-growth management are a waste of money in all but a handful of the most productive national forests — mainly those in the Douglas-fir and Southern pine regions." As for Douglas-fir, he was speaking of Western Oregon and Western Washington, only. In most places, once an old-growth stand has been clearcut, it cannot be re-grown and re-clearcut economically.

OLD-GROWTH SHOULD NEVER BE CLEARCUT

Old-growth forests are among our oldest and most valuable natural assets. They have grown, unharvested by humans, for 150 to 1,000 years, accumulating and retaining rich native diversity. Old-growth forests are almost gone.

In Oregon and Washington, outside of wildernesses and national parks, only about four percent of the old-growth remains. Much of that is in remnants too small to be considered for wilderness status. In the Tongass National Forest (Alaska), of sixteen million acres, only six million acres of old-growth survives, of which two million are already planned for clearcutting.

In the Eastern states, the percentage of remaining old-growth is even less.

In East Texas, outside of the five wildernesses and Big Thicket National Preserve, less than one percent of old-growth remains, either inside or outside the national forests. That remaining old-growth is all bottomland or lower slope hardwood, and is less than 20,000 acres out of twelve million acres of Texas timberland. Even in the 35,000 acres of East Texas Wilderness, less than 5,000 acres are old-growth, and that in scattered patches.

See Color Plate 26.

The priceless examples of old-growth on our public lands must never be cut by any method, for any purpose.

In addition to barring the Forest Service from cutting in old-growth stands, Congress should provide further protection for those stands. If the Forest Service clearcuts the surrounding timber, it will expose the old-growth groves to wind, ice storms, sun-penetration, and insect and weed invasions. Around every old-growth preserve, a buffer should be managed under the individual-tree selection system.

The federal agencies schedule clearcuts in old-growth ahead of elsewhere because old-growth timber is bigger, better, and more profitable. Where most of the old-growth is gone, as in Texas, the Forest Service plans to accelerate clearcuts in the oldest second-growth stands, with pines 70-90 years of age. The justification they give is an "imbalance" of age groups in the national forests. The Forest Service bought most of its eastern lands in 1936 when many of the pines and hardwoods were about thirty years old, coming back from heavy harvesting around the turn of the century. Those that the Forest Service has not yet cut are now tall and stout. The Forest Plans for national forests propose to speed up clearcuts of these older trees. We should limit these old second-growth stands to selection harvesting.

BUREAUCRATIC DEFENSE: "COMMERCIAL SPECIES NEED SUN!"

"Pines need sun." "Douglas-firs need sun." These are favorite cliches of clearcutting advocates.

Yet, under individual-tree selection, each felling of a mature tree leaves a big opening where its progeny can spring up.
See Color Plates 17–25. Plate 24 shows Loblolly pine regeneration.

If the opening left by one logged tree does not allow enough sunlight for a few seedlings to flourish, then the forester can mark more than one mature tree for harvesting in that opening.

Gordon Robinson, for decades the chief forester for Southern Pacific Transportation Company's California forest operation, found that the opening need be no larger than the height of a tree.

Even in the absence of logging, when a tree falls near a mature pine, its seedlings are likely to spring up in the opening.

BUREAUCRATIC DEFENSE: "WE RAISE MORE THAN ONE TREE SPECIES IN CLEARCUTS"

A number of recent forest plans claim that the management goal of clearcuts is a certain percentage of trees in the canopy other than the preferred commercial species. In the plan for several national forests in the East, the hardwood component in pine stands is "up to thirty percent." However, with the Forest Service suppressing hardwoods, hardwoods can never attain thirty percent of the canopy. In pine clearcuts over twenty years of age, burns and "stand improvement" cuttings have virtually eliminated the hardwood component in the canopy. Burns suppress most of the hardwoods and free the pines to grow above the competition. That trend intensifies with each additional burn. The slower-growing oaks and hickories cannot catch up with the pines.

At a 1985 conference sponsored by the Forest Service and CHEC in San Francisco, Max Peterson, then Chief of the Forest Service, agreed to sit with participants and discuss forestry topics. He made the usual statement, "We raise a thirty percent hardwood component in our pine stands."

We asked him to identify locations of pine stands over fifty years of age with thirty percent hardwood still remaining in the canopy. Peterson could not remember any locations, but promised to mail them to us. After prodding, he sent a study that showed no such thing.

Even if federal agencies did achieve a mixture of species in the canopy of a pine stand, in spite of the way they thin, poison, or burn, the hardwood component would not be as large as under native unmanaged conditions. Moreover, after management, the midstory, ground cover, and soil would be significantly different from the native regime.

In summary, the "goals" of federal agencies for a mixture of species in the canopy are impossible in light of the actual practices, and even if they were achieved, these goals fall far short of native diversity.

BUREAUCRATIC DEFENSE: "HARDWOODS ARE INCREASING."

An old ploy of the Forest Service is to show figures indicating that the hardwood component in the southern forests is increasing. One wonders how hardwoods could increase while the Forest Service is clearcutting nearly all stands and planting only pine in pine/hardwood stands, as well as in pine stands.

The answer lies in the way the Forest Service counts species. It measures by basal area on trees over five inches in diameter; but on smaller sizes, it counts every tree. For the first twenty years after a clearcut, hardwood stumps and roots send up multiple sprouts for each former tree. The Forest Service counts each sprout as a tree.

This explains why an increasing number of acres would have a plurality of hardwoods in the first two decades after clearcutting began in 1964. Also, for the South, since hardwood stand rotation is 120 years, compared to seventy years for Loblolly pine, and most hardwood stands in the South's national forests have not yet reached one hundred years, the hardwood acres have not yet begun to fall precipitously under even-age management. But if clearcutting continues, the fall will show up in the count.

The corollary to "hardwoods are increasing" is that commercial favorites are decreasing. Here, again, in the South, the Forest Service insistence on counting of every hardwood sprout in a clearcut makes it appear that pines are decreasing, relatively. In addition, the attrition of all timberland because of urban and pastoral expansion is resulting in a steady decline in commercial as well as non-commercial forest types.

None of these facts supports the Forest Service's ridiculous implication that its clearcutting produces a greater component of non-commercial species. Short of radical reform of Forest Service practices, the only trend that may save hardwoods is the increase in hardwood prices. If hardwoods begin to compete in the market with current commercial types, the bureaucrats may shift priorities. If the agencies learn to favor more species in each stand, this may improve wildlife and recreation, but it will not save our soil and native diversity, so long as clearcutting is the cutting method.

BUREAUCRATIC DEFENSE: "WE SHAPE CLEARCUTS."

The federal agencies boast of having landscape architects on their prescription teams, designing their timber sale boundaries to curve with the earth's contours.

If an observer concentrates on the wavy boundaries, the shaping does mollify the harshness of a clearcut, aesthetically, but does not alleviate the damage to native diversity, wildlife, recreation, and soil. It is sheer manicuring.

BUREAUCRATIC DEFENSE: "OUR CLEARCUTS ARE SMALLER."

Reducing the acreage of an individual clearcut does lessen the impacts of soil erosion and wildlife disruption, but when numerous small clearcuts cover the same total area that the larger ones would have covered, in the same rotation period, the advantages of small bites diminish almost to zero.

In some ways, smaller clearcuts are worse. For logging and site preparing equipment to reach the more numerous, more scattered, smaller clearcuts, the timber beasts must develop more roads sooner. Also, they are in there making noise with their chain saws more frequently. Recreationists can never plan a visit to an area of available timberland without the likelihood of listening to the galling whine.

All things considered, environmentalists should not make any concessions on forest plans merely to get the size of clearcuts reduced.

BUREAUCRATIC DEFENSE: "LEAVE SILVICULTURAL DECISIONS TO US PROFESSIONALS."

Back in 1976 during the NFMA hearings, before Max Peterson was appointed Chief, the main line that he followed as liaison of the Forest Service with Congress was that Congress should not handcuff our public servants from fulfilling their responsibilities in managing our national forests. These skilled professionals should be left free to take whatever measures best serve the public. All of the forests are different and cannot be confined to the same rigid rules. Silviculture is a complicated profession best left to Forest Service silviculturists who have studied it in college and have applied it for years in the field. So went the party line.

Although Peterson had started in the bureaucracy as a road engineer, his shrewdness had catapulted him to master-minding political strategy.

When Max Peterson breathed bureaucratic discretion into every pore of NFMA, he knew full well that the Forest Service had been clearcutting indiscriminately for twelve years and would continue to do so in the future. There was no real issue of flexibility of management from forest to forest. The Forest Service top brass had decided irrevocably on a course of universal even-age management. But the ruse worked. Congress accepted "agency discretion" loopholes in every key section. NFMA was riddled.

In NFMA, Congress restricted clearcutting to cases in which it would be the "optimum" method, as determined by the agency. The Forest Service has judged clearcutting to be the optimum method in virtually all its end-of-rotation harvests.

The Forest Service is like a butcher who has the usual assortment of knives and a meat axe, but who always uses a meat axe.

The Forest Service continues to use the theme: "leave it to professionals," at every challenge, including in lawsuits. They use it to justify clearcutting, SPB control cutting in wilderness, roadbuilding in roadless areas, and many other situations.

It is difficult for some people to support imposing a precise restraint on a government agency. Most of us were taught in high school that federal legislation should set broad policies, allowing room for administrative agencies to determine the implementation from time to time and place to place. Theoretically, this is a sound rule, but when an agency persists in implementing a program contrary to the wishes of Congress, then it is necessary that Congress give that agency precise and inescapable instructions. The federal agencies have brought us to that necessity with regard to clearcutting.

BUREAUCRATIC CLAIM: "WE PLANT SUPER-TREES"

The clearcutters claim that they plant seedlings from super-tree nurseries, seeded from the fastest growing and straightest trees in the forest. At first glance, this is the most plausible of the arguments for clearcutting.

Even if the seedlings grow faster and straighter, there are serious flaws in the cloning practice. Genetically, the descendants of trees that grew up on a particular site tend to be stronger and healthier than trees planted from a different site, as Gordon Robinson says in *The Forest and the Trees*.

Even if taken from similar soil and elevation, a seedling as far as fifty miles north or south of a site tends to be weaker than a tree naturally regenerated on the site.

Diversity among trees in the same species is vital in many ways. Some strains better than others can survive major changes in climate and air quality. Nobody knows which trees will better endure such major cataclysms as global warming, acid rain, increased droughts, and increased intensity of sun rays that may result from ozone depletion. We need to maintain a wide variation of each species in order to increase the chance that one strain will endure all cataclysms.

The individual trees most likely to produce descendants that will resist certain insects and diseases are those that have already resisted them. For example, consider the pines that have lived through a local infestation of Southern pine beetles, while other pines around them have died. It would be wise to leave these survivors to reseed the stand. The Forest Service is not doing that. We know it is not, because it follows a practice of cutting all green trees in a beetle spot, if commercially feasible. The agency also bulldozes the remnant pines (and other species) after the infestation, in order to clear the ground for planting of seedlings from a nursery where the trees were too young to be heavily attacked by beetles.

In any species, planting of clones reduces native diversity within the planted species, and therefore reduces the chances of that species to survive.

STRIPPED TO THEIR NAKED BOTTOMS

It becomes apparent that the federal agencies will flinch at no extremity of absurdity in an effort to keep pumping new retorts into their mill of clearcutting propaganda.

Stripped to their naked bottoms, as in the Red-cockaded woodpecker trial, Forest Service think-tankers will finally go hog wild.

Both sides had presented testimony for and against most of the excuses for clearcutting. The judge had deliberated for three months and had ruled in favor of selection management, giving the Forest Service sixty days to present a plan "consistent with the findings of the Court." To enable the agency to control hardwoods, to assure that plenty of pines would be available for the woodpeckers, the judge ordered the Forest Service to burn every two to four years "or as soon as those sites will support a burn."

Instead of filing a selection management plan, the Defendants (from the Supervisor up to the Chief) again proposed the even-age plan that the Court had rejected. Their excuse, supported by affidavits of employees, was that if you burn Loblolly or Shortleaf pine every two to four years, you will burn up all the pine seedlings that you need to keep replacing the pines that die or are harvested. They concluded that selection management would not work.

TCONR countered with affidavits of selection foresters in Alabama, Arkansas, and Texas, and of Dr. W. J. Platt, ecologist at Louisiana State University. They all told of managing all species of pine under the selection system. Louis Rainey manages close to 400,000 acres. Don Harper manages 200,000 acres. Bill Platt had managed stands at Tall Timber Research Station in Florida and had done research in Georgia where Leon Neel conducts selection management in such a way as to preserve the Red-cockaded woodpecker.

They all used frequent burning and had adequate natural regeneration of pines. They simply were flexible enough not to burn after a harvest until the new seedlings had grown tall enough to endure a burn.

So the judge overruled the Forest Service's objection to selection management.

We can be sure that the agency will conceive further objections.

PART V

What You Can Do To Save Our Forests

TARGET: THE DIVERSITY LOOPHOLE

NFMA does not tell the Forest Service to maintain native diversity. The Forest Service manipulated the House and Senate agriculture committees into riddling the diversity provision. Section 6(g) of NFMA meekly directs that the Secretary of Agriculture

"shall . . . promulgate regulations . . . that set out the process for the development and revision of land management plans, and the guidelines and standards prescribed by this subsection."

Sec. 6(g)(3) says that the regulations shall include guidelines which:

"(B) provide for diversity of plant and animal communities based on the suitability and capability of the specific land area in order to meet overall multiple-use objectives, and within the multiple-use objectives of a land management plan adopted pursuant to this section, provide, where appropriate, to the degree practicable, for steps to be taken to preserve the diversity of tree species similar to that existing in the region controlled by the plan;" (underlining supplied)

The words we have underlined are merely part of the sieve.
—— The section never says that the plant and animal communities

must be native. The Forest Service staffers now argue that a diversity of single-species tree plantations is enough to satisfy subsection 6(g)(3). In the Ouachita and Cherokee appeals, among others, the staffers point out some animals that like Shortleaf and White pines, unnatural though plantations of them are. Only one regulation of the Forest Service mentions naturalness and that one is oblique.

—— As to tree species, the above section calls for diversity "similar to that existing in the region controlled by the plan"; but does not clearly prevent leaving only a few trees of each species somewhere in the forest and cutting the rest to make way for single-species plantations.

—— The section covers only what the regulation must say about what the guidelines must say, not directly what the Forest Service must do.

—— "Guidelines" is a weak term, allowing an indefinite degree of deviation.

—— It leaves to the discretion of the Forest Service what are the "suitability and capability" of the specific land area, and the "multiple-use objectives" of the "land management plan."

In practice, the district rangers use boilerplate paragraphs to explain why they choose clearcutting, seed tree cutting, or shelterwood for each particular sale.

See excerpt.

The diversity provision of NFMA has all the effect on the Forest Service that a "Please Do Not Disturb" sign has on the dog next door when a fire engine goes by.

The remedy is for Congress to amend section 6(g) so as to require the protection of the native ecological communities, species, and intra-species genetic variants that would exist in each stand in each forest without the influence of human beings. This would permit responsible individual-tree selection, but not clearcutting.

The Forest Service will make every effort to water down the native diversity language. The agency lobbyists managed to whittle down such language in the Winding Stair Mountain National Recreation and Wilderness Area Act, Public Law 100-499, enacted in October 1988.

Perhaps the most crucial words that we need are: "in each stand." Without them, the Forest Service would continue to argue

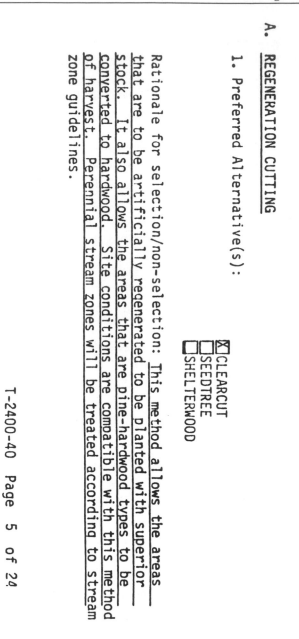

A. REGENERATION CUTTING

1. Preferred Alternative(s):

☒ CLEARCUT
☐ SEEDTREE
☐ SHELTERWOOD

Rationale for selection/non-selection: This method allows the areas that are to be artificially regenerated to be planted with superior stock. It also allows the areas that are pine-hardwood types to be converted to hardwood. Site conditions are compatible with this method of harvest. Perennial stream zones will be treated according to stream zone guidelines.

T-2400-40 Page 5 of 24

Excerpt from prescription in Sabine National Forest, Texas, Comp. 35, Tenaha District, 1988. Note that the form allows no choice of selection management.

that it provides native diversity to the forests by preserving a wilderness here, a scenic area there, and a variety of age groups in various types of cuts.

TARGET: THE CLEARCUTTING LOOPHOLE

NFMA did not order the Forest Service to reduce its clearcutting. The Forest Service again induced the congressional committees into leaving huge loopholes.

As in the case of diversity, NFMA merely directs the Secretary of Agriculture to issue regulations for the development of guidelines. Subsec. 6(g)(3) says that these regulations shall include guidelines which:

> "(F) insure that clearcutting, seed tree cutting, shelterwood cutting, and other cuts designed to regenerate an even-aged stand of timber will be used as a cutting method on National Forest System lands only where —
>
> '(i) for clearcutting, it is determined to be the optimum method, and for other such cuts, it is <u>determined</u> to be appropriate, to meet the <u>objectives</u> and <u>requirements</u> of the relevant land management <u>plan;</u>'" (Underlining supplied.)

This language includes some of the same catches as the diversity subsection plus this major gap:

—— The determination of what is the optimum method is left up to the Forest Service. As a result, the Forest Service can and does determine clearcutting to be the optimum method in virtually every stand.

—— The determination of other even-aged cuts is also left up to the Forest Service. As a result, the agency uses those other variations of clearcutting whenever it does not use simple clearcutting. The plans in all regions of the Forest Service say that the management system will be even-aged.

Almost any lawyer or any other literate person can read Sec. 6(g)(3) and surrender any hope of getting courts to order the Forest Service to reduce its clearcutting.

The plain remedy is for Congress to add a new sub-section to Section 6, placing a finite limitation on all even-age harvesting methods.

One level of limitation would be zero — no clearcutting. Unfortunately, this has no chance of passage. We could not even find a qualified forester to recommend it. Foresters generally agree that there are some stands where clearcutting is the only way to start a profitable timber crop. An example shown by the Forest Service is in the Mendocino National Forest, where, decades after a wildfire, nothing but brush and stunted pines had grown back.

The Forest Service argues that national forests differ, so each supervisor should be free to determine what policies should prevail. This argument is inconsistent with the Forest Service policy that even-age management shall prevail in almost all national forests, nationwide.

If we leave each forest supervisor to fix his own clearcutting maximum, we are not likely to obtain firm, protective limits.

In seeking a common denominator, the author asked the Committee of Scientists, appointed by the Secretary of Agriculture in 1976, what was the highest fraction of available commercial timberland in any national forest that could be silviculturally justified for clearcutting. The highest any of them could come up with was one-fifth. Some environmental groups have endorsed a clearcutting limit of one-tenth of the available commercial timberland in any national forest. By now, the Forest Service has already clearcut beyond that theoretical level in many national forests.

The proposed limit is absolute. Once one-tenth of the timberland had been placed under even-age management, no more clearcutting in any of its variations could ever be done anywhere in that forest, not even the portion already clearcut. Nobody has come up with another alternative that would remove all loopholes, as this one does.

The one-tenth maximum gives the Forest Service some discretion in forests that have not yet been clearcut to that extent. The Service can stop itself at any number below that. Therefore, the one-tenth maximum is reasonable, as well as being strict.

TARGET: THE FOREST SERVICE HIERARCHY

The Forest Service is so adept at avoiding congressional attempts to control it that we must not rely on legislative reform, alone. We need thoroughgoing administrative reforms as well.

The Forest Service is a quasi-military hegemony. Gifford Pinchot brought many of its elements across from the autocratic bureaucracy of Frederick the Great of Prussia. Pinchot founded a tightly-knit, tightly-governed, uniformed, partly armed, heavily equipped corps. "The Mission, a Case of Family Fidelity," B. W. Twight, National Forest Mission Symposium, San Francisco, CA, December 14, 1984.

Its chief, now and historically, is a skillful administrator and shrewd politician, accustomed to having his own way, to defending his people, and staying on the right side of the timber industry, his main constituency. He also knows when and how to appease those who might cause congressional intervention.

TARGET: THE CHIEF AND DEPUTY

In January 1987, Max Peterson resigned as Forest Service Chief. The Reagan administration, as pre-arranged, appointed Dale Robertson to replace him, and George Leonard to fill Robertson's former position as Deputy Chief. These two veterans are smoother yet than Peterson. Robertson wrote to his regional foresters on September 8, 1988: ". . . take an open-minded approach in identifying and evaluating silvicultural systems and cutting practices. We should seek opportunities to reduce clearcutting when other alternatives meet our land management objectives." But he has yet to overturn any of the seventy or more forest plans that call for indiscriminate even-age management.

The chief is appointed and supervised by the Secretary of Agriculture, who is appointed and supervised by the President. Only with the backing of the President can the people obtain a Forest Service Chief who will reform the Forest Service.

The people must elect a President committed to reform. The time to obtain such a commitment is during a presidential campaign. This will require voters, workers, and contributions.

The goal is replacement of the top brass of the Forest Service, including the Chief, with responsible administrators, followed by a rapid assertion and continued maintenance of dominance over the entire bureaucracy.

By the next election, the final plans for most of the national forests will be in operation or under administrative appeal or in court. Lacking congressionally mandated reform, the people and the courts would have to force the Forest Service to reform those forest plans before it would ever shift to selection harvesting. Congress, on the other hand, might amend NFMA long before the administrative and court appeals could be concluded.

Proponents of reform will not be satisfied merely to replace

Dale Robertson as Chief. There are too many under him who would be just as pro-clearcutting and just as slick. Reform must be sweeping, at and near the top.

TARGET: BLM, BIA, AND THE MILITARY

In addition to owning about 358 million acres of desert and mountains, the Bureau of Land Management has about two million acres of available commercial forest. These are part of BLM's O and C (Oregon and California) lands.

The agency is systematically clearcutting its timberland, under even less legislative restraint than the Forest Service.
See photo "Nude Mountain."

A good way to restrict BLM would be to transfer its O and C lands to the national forests when Congress strengthens NFMA. NFMA amendments would then cover the former BLM timberland. Otherwise, it would be necessary to amend the Federal Land Policy and Management Act that governs BLM.

The Bureau of Indian Affairs, U.S. Fish and Wildlife Service, Army, Navy, and Air Force own the other fifteen million acres of federal timberland. To stop their clearcutting, Congress will have to amend the laws governing them.

LIMIT OF THIS BOOK

There are other abuses in the management of our federal forests, including but not limited to, excessive road-building, sales below costs, grazing excesses, failure to designate and protect qualified forests as wilderness or scenic areas, damages by mining, and use of biocides over and above the uses that Congress will prevent by ending clearcutting. Other evils, perhaps even more far-reaching, are the Brush Disposal Act of 1915, the Knutson-Vandenberg Act of 1930, and the provisions in NFMA relating to timber salvage sales. Under these laws, the more timber that the Forest Service sells, the more dollars flow into its budget, regardless of whether receipts on such sales are below costs. We must eliminate all these scourges. But this book does not attempt to cover them further.

Furthermore, operations and maintenance of each resource — recreation, fish and wildlife, water, timber, range, and minerals — should be funded out of a portion of the net receipts produced by that resource. This will give managers the incentive to maximize

"Nude Mountain," Oregon, 1972. By Trygve P. Steen.
    The Bureau of Land Management, which owns four million acres of public tim-
berland in the west, can equal the Forest Service in scouring capacity.

net returns from national forest management. Fees at market prices should be collected for all resources. Given that their funding will come out of receipts, managers will be less likely to sell resources below cost. These reforms will enable the first three resources to receive their fair share of the pie. They will also make it unnecessary for Congress to continue to appropriate funds for most Forest Service activities. Appropriations will still be needed for endangered species, watershed protection and research, but not for timber production and logging road construction.

In "The Citizens' Guide to Reforming the Forest Service," *Forest Watch*, September 1988, Randal O'Toole has discussed these reforms, favoring those that depend on market economics, and begrudging those that depend on making rules for the Forest Service to follow. As a forest economist, O'Toole believes that economic reforms will be sufficient, except that we will need to maintain and strengthen the Endangered Species Act, to enforce the Clean Water Act against the timber agencies, and to compensate displaced timber workers with a fund.

O'Toole recommends exemption of the Forest Service from the National Environmental Policy Act, except as to rare species and habitats and clean water. This change would deprive citizens of badly needed leverage to enforce sound forest practices.

Many environmentalists are willing to try O'Toole's economic reforms, but do not think they, alone, would induce the federal agencies to give up clearcutting and even-age management. Federal clearcutters are too short-sighted and biased to switch to selection for market and budget reasons, alone. Besides, in the short run, they can sell just as much timber under even-age as selection management. Nor would they leave our remaining old growth standing unless required specifically to do so. People trained to cut timber are inclined toward cutting whatever will sell. Moreover, at least in some national forests, it will be decades before most people will pay fees for recreation that they have always obtained gratis up to now.

O'Toole tends to be oversold on the curative powers of market economics when applied to giant bureaucracies. So long as the federal government is there to bail them out for misadventures, and to cover their insurance and retirement pay, timber agency employees are likely to place their biases ahead of the free market, and even ahead of some budgetary inducements.

Clearcutting causes more total damage than any other forest evil. It deserves higher priority than any other reform. In no event will most clearcutting opponents rely upon purely economic solutions.

FULL FOREST REFORM

Some citizen groups have their hearts set so firmly on saving the remaining patches of old growth in the Pacific Northwest that they cannot focus on the fate of the second-growth forests in between those patches.

Other groups see sales below cost, or Knutson-Vandenberg, or road-building, or the skewed Forest Service budget as the root of the evil.

Then, too, some people want to save particular animals, like mountain lions or timber wolves, or Red-cockaded woodpeckers.

If unified with all the people who abhor clearcutting, these groups have the energy and resources to move Congress into action.

They could all join forces on a comprehensive bill or packet of bills that would accomplish full forest reform. Efforts are beginning toward this goal.

WHAT CAN YOU DO?

In Congress, the House Agriculture Committee, Subcommittee on Forests, has held oversight hearings and plans more. That subcommittee's counterpart in the Senate is planning such hearings. Any citizen who wants to express views on clearcutting reform may write to:

> Hon. Chairman,
> Forest Subcommittee, House Agriculture Committee
> House Office Building
> Washington, D.C. 20515

One may also write to one's own congressman, same address.

One may ask them to end clearcutting and require preservation of native diversity on our federal forests. The writer should tell them why.

Another way to take action is to lend this book to others, asking them to write, likewise.

PART VI

Regional Glimpses
of Holocaust

THE FIRST COURT TEST SINCE NFMA:
EVEN-AGE VERSUS SELECTION MANAGEMENT

In 1987, two Forest Service biologists drafted a field report showing that in the preceding four years, Red-cockaded woodpeckers had lost almost half their active clans ("colonies") in three of the four national forests in Texas, as follows:

Angelina N.F.,   42% decline.
Davy Crockett N.F.,   41% decline.
Sabine N.F.,   50% decline.

The report implied that the ongoing clearcutting of these forests was a cause of the decline.

The Forest Service later found similar results in Sam Houston National Forest. The authors of the 1987 Texas report cite other reports showing that a decline is occurring "throughout the birds' range."

See Color Plate 29.

This crash of an endangered species occurred simultaneously with two major Forest Service actions:

1. The heaviest buffer-cutting in history, in those same four years, in a vain campaign to "protect" Red-cockaded woodpecker colony trees and privately-owned pines from Southern pine beetles.

These cuts often reduced "preferred foraging habitats" previously set aside for RCWs.

2. Pervasive clearcutting sales between preferred foraging habitats, and often right up to, and sometimes around, Red-cockaded woodpecker colony reserves.

The colony "reserves" were the pines in which RCW's have dug cavities for nesting and roosting, plus 200-foot zones around them. The "preferred foraging habitats" were 125-acre minimum areas of pines that include at least forty percent over sixty years of age.

There may be other undisclosed causes of the crash, but there is every reason to hypothesize that the beetle-cutting and clearcutting are at least contributing factors.

The Forest Service was selling timber up to and around RCW colonies and then paying heavy equipment operators to bulldoze all the remaining vegetation. Maps 1, 2, and 3 are maps that the Forest Service included in its solicitation for bids on "Mechanical site preparation" of 674 acres in the Raven Ranger District, Sam Houston National Forest, on July 11, 1986. The small circles around "R" indicate Red-cockaded woodpecker colonies. The hashlines indicate the areas to be sheared, raked, and windrowed by heavy equipment. They had all been clearcut.

The solicitation says: "The contract areas were infested with the southern pine beetle in the summer of 1985, and have subsequently been partially logged over by salvage operations."

To the Forest Service and its timber customers "salvage" is a euphemism that includes more uninfested than infested trees. The buyers of "salvage" timber make good money out of it. The Forest Service loses heavily.

The Forest Service has made numerous such sales, and has followed them up with massive shearing or chopping contracts.

The smartest people in the Forest Service realize that the best answer to the pine beetle problem is a change in timber management practices. This, of course, would incidentally benefit the Red-cockaded woodpecker by replacing the buffer-cutting program that destroys their foraging habitat. In "Managing Southern Forests to Reduce Southern Pine Beetles," the Forest Service Core Team in early 1986 found that increased density of pines is an important contributing factor in the massive SPB epidemic of 1983–1986. Its first conclusion was:

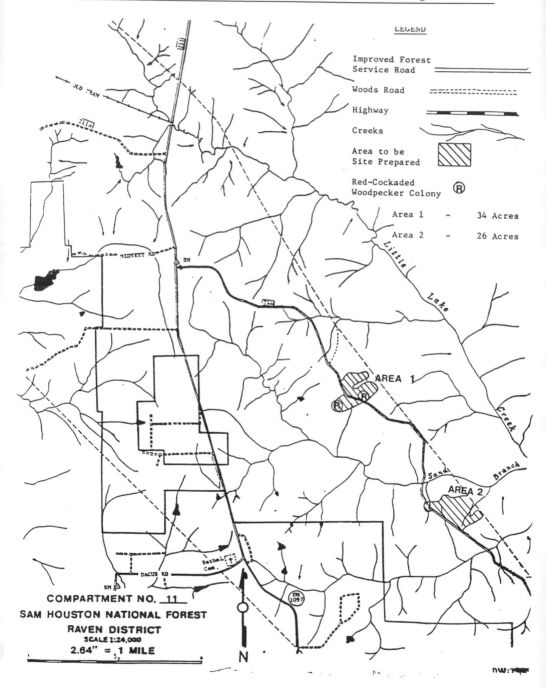

LEGEND

Improved Forest Service Road

Woods Road

Highway

Creeks

Area to be Site Prepared

Red-Cockaded Woodpecker Colony Ⓡ

Area 1   –   34 Acres

Area 2   –   26 Acres

AREA 1

AREA 2

COMPARTMENT NO. 11
SAM HOUSTON NATIONAL FOREST
RAVEN DISTRICT
SCALE 1:24,000
2.64" = 1 MILE

N

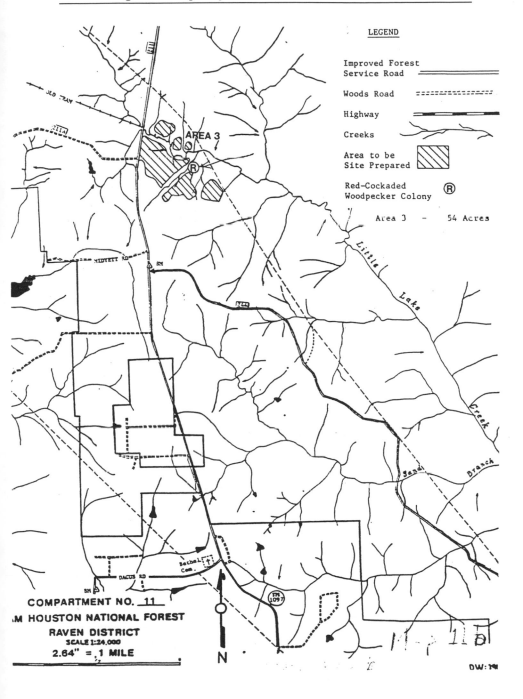

LEGEND

Improved Forest
Service Road

Woods Road

Highway

Creeks

Area to be
Site Prepared

Red–Cockaded
Woodpecker Colony ®

Area 3 — 54 Acres

AREA 3

COMPARTMENT NO. 11
M HOUSTON NATIONAL FOREST
RAVEN DISTRICT
SCALE 1:24,000
2.64" = 1 MILE

N

DW:1

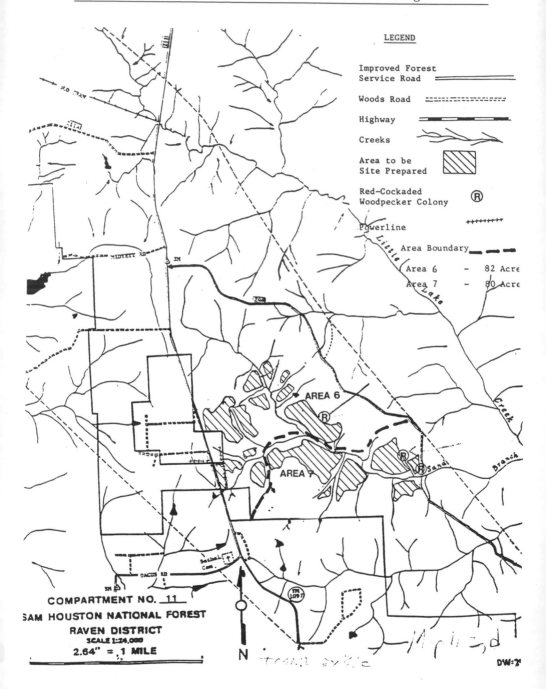

"This will involve some major changes in current management policies and practices. We believe that:
— The greatest long-term benefits can be achieved by actions that will significantly reduce acreage of mature, overmature, and dense stands."

Although the Core Team did not say so, selection management with native diversity is the best way to prevent density of pines. After the 1986 finding, the Forest Service stepped up its thinning operations, but continued its buffer-cutting policy.

Directly addressing the effect of buffer-cutting on Red-cockaded woodpeckers, a Houston ornithologist, Dr. Robert W. McFarlane, wrote an analysis of the few records the Forest Service has published on buffer-cutting to "protect" RCW colonies. His analysis shows that buffer-cutting has provided no more protection than would be expected without buffer-cutting. He concluded that, since buffer-cutting is not shown to provide any protection, but definitely reduces foraging habitat, it inflicts a net harm on RCW.

Likewise, in its timber business, the Forest Service continued to make numerous clearcut sales up to, and often around, Red-cockaded woodpecker colonies.

You can see an example in Map 4 from the Forest Service prospectus of December 11, 1986. Stands 2 and 6 on the northern boundary were sold for clearcutting around RCW colonies. Note that clearcutting is so common that they do not even bother to say what kind of cut it is. Everybody just knows it is a clearcut, unless otherwise indicated, as in Stand 4 which was sold for commercial thinning ("I.C.," intermediate cut). Thinning is not so harmful to RCW, if it is done with care for the ecosystem, as in selection management.

Although Forest Service regulations required at least 125 acres of preferred foraging habitat for each Red-cockaded woodpecker clan, this was often stretched out for some distance from the nesting tree. In an attempt to make enough feeding trips to sustain their growing nestlings, the adults often fly across intervening clearcuts, thereby exposing themselves to predators that pounce upon them in flight or follow them to the nest-hole and gobble the nestlings.

Like most endangered species, Red-cockaded woodpeckers have a peculiarity that limits their potential for survival. They are not inclined to move their colony to a new area under any conditions. They'd rather die than switch. This may be because they nest

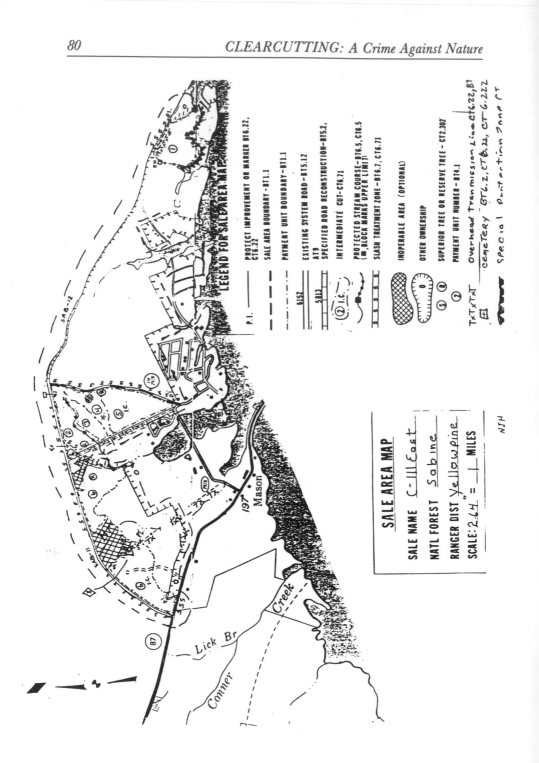

LEGEND FOR SALE AREA MAP

PROTECT IMPROVEMENT OR MARKER-BT6.22, CT6.22

P.I. ——— SALE AREA BOUNDARY - BT1.1

PAYMENT UNIT BOUNDARY - BT1.1

EXISTING SYSTEM ROAD - BT5.12
AT9

0152   SPECIFIED ROAD RECONSTRUCTION - BT5.2.

5813   INTERMEDIATE CUT - CT6.71

(P) I.C.   PROTECTED STREAM COURSE - BT6.5, CT6.5
(IN BLOCK MARKS UPPER LIMIT)

SLASH TREATMENT ZONE - BT6.7, CT6.71

INOPERABLE AREA (OPTIONAL)

OTHER OWNERSHIP

(S) (R)   SUPERIOR TREE OR RESERVE TREE - CT2.302

(2)   PAYMENT UNIT NUMBER - BT4.1

T×T×T×T   Overhead transmission Line - CT6.22, BT

⊞   Cemetery BT6.2, CT6.11, CT 6.222

〰〰   Special Protection Zone CT

SALE AREA MAP

SALE NAME   C-III East

NATL FOREST   Sabine

RANGER DIST   Yellowpine

SCALE: 2.64 " = 1 MILES

NJH

in cavities in diseased but living pines. With their small bills, RCW sometimes take months to drill a new cavity in such hard scrabble.

For many years, an RCW clan (2 to 9 birds) can endure clear-cutting. They do it by expanding their foraging territory to substitute more distant or less nourishing pine stands for those that have been cut. But finally, two things happen. All the potential expansion habitat is clearcut, and all the available cavity trees die within the colony reserve. Those events have hit home in the last few years, hence the sudden sharp decline in RCW population. Now, let us summarize what happened after the 1987 field report. The authors, Dr. Richard Conner and Dr. Craig Rudolph, of the Forest Service Experiment Station at Nacogdoches, Texas, submitted the first draft to the Supervisor of National Forests in Texas. The Supervisor called in the authors to adjust their findings. They had some agreements and disagreements. The authors were asked to go to Atlanta, Georgia, for a discussion with the Regional Forester.

Meanwhile, either Conner or Rudolph circulated the draft for peer review. One of the reviewers felt that the Forest Service was suppressing the study too long, under the alarming circumstances. Texas Committee on Natural Resources obtained possession, and added a new Endangered Species Act claim to an existing lawsuit. Sierra Club and The Wilderness Society joined in the claim. The feathers had hit the fan.

The trial began on February 29, 1988. A principle issue was the feasibility of selection management. Randal O'Toole, forest economist from Eugene, Oregon, testified that the 1987 Land and Resource Management Plan for the four forests showed substantial costs for site preparation under even-age management, and for planting after clearcutting. He told how selection management would involve no such costs. Selection depends upon natural regeneration, thereby avoiding site preparation and planting.

Bill Carroll, of Huntsville, Texas, consulting forester, testified that selection management is feasible throughout the South, and that many landowners, large and small, use it profitably.

As rebuttal, the Defendants presented the testimony of their full-time expert, Dr. James Baker, of Crossett, Arkansas. He testified that even-age management was superior under the net present value standard. The attorney for TCONR asked him, in cross-examination, which system was superior under the cost-efficiency standard. Baker said selection management was more cost-efficient than even-age, and produced about the same amount of sawlogs. He said it would take twelve to twenty years to convert some stands completely from even-age to selection.

In his decision of June 17, 1988, Judge Robert M. Parker, U.S. District Court, Tyler, Texas, found that selection management is better for the woodpecker and more cost efficient. He also found that under selection management the pines are kept less dense, and therefore, less susceptible to Southern pine beetles.

After the trial, Judge Parker enjoined the Forest Service from making any more timber sales involving clearcutting or its variations within 1,200 meters of any Red-cockaded woodpecker colonies. That amounts to 1,100 acres for each of the 180 remaining colonies in the four national forests in Texas. That comes to 200,000 acres; but the total acreage would be somewhat less than that because some of the protection zones overlap. The total land in the four forests is about 600,000 acres.

Judge Parker ordered that future harvesting in the protection zones must be by selection management, and must leave uncut a large component of the oldest pines as potential cavity trees.

This case was the first court test of pervasive clearcutting versus selection management. There is no reason why the court's findings of feasibility of selection management would not be applicable to any region of the nation. That destroys the Forest Service's main stated objection to the selection alternative.

This case also involved the first court skirmish over Knutson-Vandenberg (see Part IV, Why Do Bureaucrats Really Insist on Clearcutting?). O'Toole testified that the Forest Service allocated large sums from timber sales to its KV account for site preparation and planting. He said this provision invites a bias for clearcutting. TCONR also introduced Forest Service documents exhorting staff to "maximize" the allocating of KV frcm timber sales in order to fund more hardwood removal on Red-cockaded woodpecker colonies.

In spite of such powerful evidence as to the pro-clearcutting bias of KV, the court did not make a finding on that point. However, it is probable that the court did consider the KV bias when he ordered the Forest Service to shift to selection management.

Within a week after Judge Parker's decision of June 17, the Supervisor of National Forests in Texas, a Defendant in the case, had the gall to make a series of public claims that the decision would reduce timber sales and might have a severe impact on the economy of East Texas. The loggers who buy timber heavily from the national forests picked up the cry. The Texas Farm Bureau jumped on the wagon and grabbed the reins. They hitched up Republican U.S. Senator Phil Gramm to oppose the decision. All of them chanted, "Jobs, jobs, jobs." Loggers circled their "wagons" (haulers) around the Supervisor's headquarters. They flaunted huge signs and posters bearing epithets such as "Cow Pies For Fritz." The Supervisor met with them consolingly. Although he had been implying that the court had thwarted his sales, he assured the loggers that he would resume his sales the very next week. They would have to be thinnings, instead of clearcuts.

The only refreshing sight near the loggers' trucks was a small group of environmentalists. Kristi Stevens carried a poster, "Extinct Is Forever."

See photo "One Bold Soul," July 1988.

Between the court decision and the circling of the trucks, I had toured ten major towns in the timber belt, explaining to audiences and media that the testimony and court judgment showed selection management to be as productive as even-age. I had explained it to the Farm Bureau twice, and to loggers four times. Some of the media had published my point that the judge had not stopped timber harvesting, but had merely ordered a change in methods. The Forest Service loggers, and Farm Bureau leaders, including a recently retired Forest Service "silviculturist," refused to acknowledge that fact. They hued to their line that the judge had stopped logging in the national forests.

In Seattle and Boise, in the same period, loggers were staging truck caravans against environmental proposals, and were chanting, "Jobs." This is a national tactic.

The judge was not cowed. He had given the Defendants sixty days to provide a plan consistent with his rulings. Intransigently, they refused. Instead, they repeated their strategy for shelterwood cutting, modified by letting some of the shelterwood pines live on. On October 20, the judge said that the Forest Service plan "deviates fundamentally from the Court's order." He overruled that plan and declared his June 17 injunction as permanent and final.

As this book went to press, the Defendants gave notice of appeal to the U.S. Circuit Court at New Orleans. Three of its thirty-three judges will receive the assignment of deciding the fate of the

"One Bold Soul" Lufkin, Texas, 1988, by Stephen Mengst.

Red-cockaded woodpecker. The appeals judges are bound by law to give weight to the trial court's finding as to the truth of what the witnesses testified. But that principle does not limit them from reversing the injunction on other grounds, as occurred in TCONR's first clearcutting case in 1978. The inside story of that lawsuit is told in this author's first book, *Sterile Forest*.

In 1989, under the threat of another lawsuit, the Forest Service ordered a cessation of further even-age logging sales within 3/4 mile of Red-cockaded woodpecker colonies in all but three national forests from Louisiana to Virginia.

CONFRONTATION ON THE GEORGE WASHINGTON

We stopped on a pleasant slope under the cool canopy of seventy-foot-tall White, Chestnut, Black, and Scarlet oaks. In the mid-story were some Red maples, Serviceberries, and Sassafras. The ground was covered with their leaves, through which clumps of blueberries had emerged and were about to blossom.

It was a relief from standing in the hot mid-June sun 200 yards downhill and listening to the Forest Service Ranger and the Virginia Commission of Game and Inland Fisheries biologist tell us about the values of a "wildlife clearing" overgrown with three-foot-high White clover, a species brought to this country from Europe.

To get there from Washington, D.C. we had ridden a chartered bus for 1 1/2 hours — across the curling Shenandoah, and over a verdant ridge of the Massanutten Range.

"Why would you want to clearcut this stand?" we asked the Ranger.

"Because it is already even-aged," he replied with absolute confidence. "The best way to harvest a stand that's all one age is to clearcut it and start it over with vigorous young growth."

"These trees are all the same age?" asked a woman in our group. "They are many sizes."

"Yes," I said, anxious to steer the conversation to the main point, "but some have been suppressed by faster-growing neighbors. The point is that this stand could be harvested by individual-tree selection and thus we could avoid the devastation of clearcutting."

"It was clearcut eighty-five years ago," the Ranger countered, "and where is the devastation you're claiming?"

"But eighty-five years ago," I replied, "the Forest Service

didn't own it. In those days, nobody came in with site preparation and cut down all the trees that were left after the clearcut. Nobody came in and thinned out the Chestnut oaks and other species that bring a lower price."

In the middle of my response, the resourceful ranger pulled out his core-driller, and began to core a White oak tree fourteen inches in diameter, diverting the subject back to his own point. He then cored another White oak half the size of the first.

"Count the rings," he challenged triumphantly. I realized that he had set up this stop, probably these very two trees. He had led us into Stand 18, of Compartment 111, off the logging road although he had promised to take us up the road to Stand 15, and then to Stand 19, scheduled for early clearcutting. Stand 18 was not scheduled for clearcutting in the next ten years.

In spite of all the Ranger's arguments for clearcutting, he later admitted this was a stand that would probably go to "group selection," in groups of 1/4 to 2 acres, too large for us, but not as bad as a clearcut.

Two of our group counted the rings, about 79 to 82, indicating those ages. By that time people were strolling in all directions.

A conservation forester, Al Sample, was with us. He described to the Ranger how some trees could be cut individually and in groups, and seedlings could regenerate in the openings, so that ultimately this could become an uneven-age stand. Such a stand could produce the same amount of timber as by clearcutting, without the damage to soil and recreation.

The Ranger kept coming back with his stock refrain, "Clearcutting is the only method that will work here. I know. I've been doing it."

I kept asking when we were going to climb on up to Stands 15 and 19.

Finally, the Ranger led us back to the road and up the hill. The road was straight and well-ditched. No trees were close enough to shade us. After about fifteen minutes of ascent, we reached the lower edge of Stand 15, a 1978 clearcut now grown back into a thicket of oaks and Virginia pine about ten feet tall. You could not see into them beyond the front row of trees.

The Ranger stopped on the road and told us how he planned to send crews into the stand with chain saws to cut the less desirable species of trees, and some of the desirable ones. The prescriptions also called for herbicides. The Ranger called our attention to the blossoms on the legumes that the Forest Service had planted along the road to hold the soil and to feed deer.

Not a soul in the group attempted to penetrate as much as one step into the sapling-clogged clearcut.

"Let's go on to the stand scheduled to have this happen to it," someone said. But others still had questions, so the Ranger answered them. Ultimately, we induced him to go on up the road toward the uncut stand. But after about fifteen minutes of walking between the two halves of the clearcut, he said it was still about another fifteen minutes away. Our leader said our time was up. We returned downhill to the bus.

On the way back to Washington, I reflected on my visit to the George Washington in late April, when that great wilderness gentleman, Ernie Dickerman, had led us behind his mountain home into the mixed hardwood/pine groves and terrible clearcuts on the Allegheny Mountains portion of the national forest west of the Massanutten Mountains.

That time, the white-blossoming Serviceberry trees ("Shad") were brightening the woods like cloud-wisps, and the deep green of the White pines (named for their wood) provided the only verdure. In some groves, these pines grow to huge proportions, rivaled only by mighty oaks, whose buds were beginning to swell. Trout lilies were blooming prolifically along a creek, but clearcutters in the adjoining stand had pushed slash within thirty feet of the creek. Scarcely a ridge was free of the pockmarks of clearcutting. At places, erosion was clearly visible.

As in the eastern half of the George Washington, the Forest Service is thinning the western half in favor of commercial tree species.

Altogether, under its new Plan, the Forest Service is clearcutting eighty-six percent of the "suitable lands" (new Forest Service euphemism for "available commercial" timber). That is only a slight reduction from the percent in the draft plan. The other fourteen percent is divided between shelterwood (two-stage clearcut) and group selection. At least twenty percent of the clearcuts would be planted to pine, mainly White pine, including on slopes where more hardwoods than pines previously grew.

Such aggressive clearcutting would reduce the populations of many species that prefer shade, including Cucumber and Umbrella magnolia, Serviceberry, Bloodroot and Trillium, along with animal species that need old trees, like Black bear, Flying squirrel, and virtually all the woodpeckers. There are no places in the region where these species are increasing. The total effect is a steep reduction in native diversity from a regional aspect.

See Color Plate 1.

Standing in the way of such desecration were nine citizen groups that filed or intervened in administrative appeals from the George Washington Land and Resource Management Plan, including the Natural Resources Defense Council, Sierra Club and The Wilderness Society. This is one of the most far-reaching appeals, covering many other subjects as well as clearcutting.

After the citizens filed their appeal against the Regional Forester, he requested that it be suspended to permit further analysis. The Chief complied. Neither of them granted a stay of clearcutting sales during the anticipated two years of delay. This is one more instance where the Forest Service has suspended an appeal with the effect of stretching its years of clearcutting.

FLORIDA AND LONGLEAF PINE

In the three national forests in Florida, the Forest Service plan calls for almost total even-age management, mostly single-stage clearcutting. This is a continuation, at an accelerated pace, of what they had already been doing there. In the openings thus created, they generally plant either Slash or Longleaf pine.

Dr. Bruce Means, of the Coastal Plains Institute at Tallahassee, stated that these even-age practices would drastically reduce native diversity. "Site preparation silviculture is the death-knell of remnant longleaf communities," he said, referring specifically to mechanical disturbance of the soil, and planting of pines in tight rows, including Slash pine on sites natural for Longleafs. These statements appear in his comments of June 21, 1985, on the draft plan, but are also true of the final plan.

The Longleaf pine community in Florida national forests is significantly different from that in Texas. In Florida, *Aristida stricta* is its major grass. Texas has none of that species of wiregrass, but has a great deal of Pinehills bluestem. Overall there is about a fifty percent difference in plant composition. So it is vital that we save both.

The Apalachicola, Osceola, and Ocala contain habitats for

over 500 species of vertebrates, thousands of species of invertebrates, and around 2,000 species of plants. The Forest Service has selected only eight vertebrates under the concept of "management indicator species" a yardstick for its timber practices. For most of the acreage, it selected species that can utilize clearcuts after the weeds enter. These indicator species are deer, bear, turkey, and quail. As a result, the Forest Service virtually ignores the habitat needs of most of the plants and animals that cannot survive in clearcuts, these being the ones whose habitats are vanishing rapidly.

Dr. Means questions whether even Black bear really benefit by the "wildlife" clearcutting that the Forest Service is doing.

A native Longleaf pine/wiregrass community is probably the most biologically diverse of the national forests in Florida, mainly because of its rich groundcover of ferns, Pitcherplants, orchids, death-camasses, and a myriad of other plants and animals. Forest Service personnel, as well as private timber companies, are reducing the Longleaf acreage. Where once it was sixty million, it is now less than ten million acres, of which 700,000 are in national forests from Florida to Texas, (one-third in Florida).

But even where they return the Longleaf pine in the overstory, the even-age managers are decimating the native diversity below the canopy. The worst phase of it is site preparation, especially by shearing or chopping with heavy equipment. This opens the ground to weeds. Weeds replace the native plant and animal composition.

See Color Plate 3.

As Means puts it at p. 3: ". . . even age silviculture is destroying alpha, beta, and gamma diversity by converting species-rich longleaf pine locally adapted communities to unnaturally densely stocked, closed canopy, nursery stock pine tree farms." Means noted that selection management preserves native diversity (p. 23).

Some of the largest existing populations of endangered Red-cockaded woodpeckers are on the Florida national forests, with the Apalachicola the best hope of saving the species. Wholesale clearcutting leaves open spaces through which the adults must fly to reach their colonies for roosting and for feeding the young. While crossing these clearcuts, the birds are especially vulnerable to hawks, and can be observed by other species that then maraud their nests.

Dr. Phillip D. Doerr recommended against clearcutting in Longleaf pine sites in order to better preserve the Red-cockaded woodpecker (Comments on the Draft Plan for Land and Resource Management, National Forests in Texas, next to last page). The Forest Service did not follow his recommendation.

The Forest Service's Florida Plan even calls for clearcutting all bottomland hardwood stands, including the vanishing beech/magnolia plant community. Clearcutting absolutely demolishes that community for decades, if not centuries.

The National Wildlife Federation is spearheading the administrative appeal from the Forest Service's final plan for Florida. Unless they win, the national forests in Florida are doomed for "multiple use," as the Forest Service interprets that phrase.

MARK TWAIN NATIONAL FOREST, MISSOURI

Once clearcut, the green drapery of oaks, hickories, and pines cloaking southeastern Missouri will need a century to cover again the rocky scrabble of the Ozark Mountains. Nevertheless, the Forest Service is engaged in clearcutting all but 100,000 of the 1.25 million acres of timberland in Mark Twain National Forest.

See Color Plate 8.

This massive clearcutting is leveling not only the mature White oaks, Red oaks, Black oaks, and Shortleaf pines that go to market but also the mature Mockernut hickories, Sugar maples, Black gums, Red maples, Blackjack oaks, sassafrasses, dogwoods, and redbuds that do not go to market, and the Farkleberries, Spicebushes, Solomon seals, hydrangeas, and other flowering plants that are crushed during the cutting.

Within about a year, the Service contracts for site preparation — sawing down any surviving woody stems. In five to ten years, they hire another contractor to cut or to poison a substantial portion of the shoots that have sprung up abundantly from the stumps, so that the oaks or pines that remain can grow faster.

In some stands, the Service plants Shortleaf pines eight feet apart, even where they formerly occupied only seventeen percent of those stands. To maintain a higher proportion, the Service will have to cut and to poison the hardwoods around these pinelings repeatedly.

All the damage and expense of these clearcutting practices is unnecessary. The national forests can produce at least as much timber with at least as good a wildlife habitat by single-tree selection management, the way Leo Drey does it. Drey is selectively managing 153,000 acres in the same region, including inholdings surrounded by federal clearcuts. Drey thereby avoids the costs of site preparation and planting, and preserves natural diversity.

We visited with Ray Culpepper, contractor who was clearcutting an oak/hickory/pine stand on national forest land. He volunteered that he hated to clearcut but that was the only way the Forest Service would sell its timber. He said he had once purchased timber from Leo Drey, on the selection basis, and that was the way he preferred to cut.

We followed Forest Service roads to see one of their infrequent seed tree cuts. En route, we counted fifty-three federal clearcuts of eighteen to forty acres each.

Since Forest Service timber sales are priced below the cost of making the sale, they soften the market for Mr. Drey and other private timber growers. Nevertheless, Drey makes a profit from his sales.

The Forest Service clearcuts were on varying slopes up to at least 40 degrees, often eroding in spite of construction of water bars.

On the plus side, the 1986 Forest Service Plan does allow for 100,000 acres of uneven age management, not yet under way. Of this, 30,000 acres are in recognizedly sensitive acres, and the remainder are along permanent streams. In NFMA, Congress directed the Forest Service to protect these riparian areas.

OKLAHOMA AND ARKANSAS

In the Ouachita National Forest of Oklahoma and Arkansas, America's first national forest, the Forest Service is in the process of clearcutting (and occasionally seed-tree cutting) all of its timber stands. For the next fifty years, the Final Forest Plan of 1986 calls for continuing the clearcutting of 844,000 of the 1,085,000 acres of available commercial timber. They could schedule the remainder for clearcutting in the next plan, ten or twenty years from now.

They have already clearcut 268,000 acres since they began the desecration in 1968.

See Color Plate 10.

They are logging on slopes almost as steep as they come in the Ouachita Mountains — even above thirty degrees. Many of the clearcuts will not grow back to sawlogs size for centuries. They are mining trees like metals — gone forever.

A forester marks the trees to be sold, especially the shortleaf pines. The Forest Service advertises and sells them to the highest (or only) bidder. The purchaser sends in its own crew to chain saw, skid, load, and haul out the marked trees, leaving the soil mashed and rutted, and the remaining vegetation in a shambles.

Within one to five years, the Forest Service sends in workers, generally under contract, to get rid of the remaining vegetation. On gentle slopes they usually bulldoze down everything and rip up the roots, except for an occasional hardwood left for wildlife. Sometimes they burn all the slash. At other sites, they frequently poison the surviving trees by spreading certain herbicides on the soil around them, or by hand-spraying, or by injecting with a sharp axe or other blade.

On a majority of sites, the Forest Service follows up a site preparation by planting shortleaf pines (sometimes loblolly pines). On seed-tree cuts, they wait a few years to see if the new pine seedlings are numerous enough. If not, they plant new seedlings.

Every few years after the planting, they poison or burn so as to kill or keep down all "undesirabale vegetation," or "brush," as they often refer to young oaks, maples, gums, dogwoods, and other broad-leaf species.

Private companies, especially Weyerhauser, are engaged in similar wholesale clearcutting on huge acreages.

Pervasive clearcuts have increased soil erosion and loss of nutrients. The sediment runs off into the Ouachita and Fourche Rivers, silting up dams that supply water for the people of Hot Springs and Little Rock, and deteriorating their water quality.

All this "even-age management" eliminates the natural life systems, including the following associations (species named in order of density):

Valley-bottom floodplain: Sugar maple, Bitternut hickory, Sweet gum, Ironwood, Shumard oak, White oak, Shortleaf pine, and in places, American beech.

North-facing slopes: Mockernut hickory, Linden, White oak, Cucumber magnolia.

Lower north-facing slopes: Shumard oak, Mockernut hickory, Red maple, Black gum, Shortleaf pine, White oak.

South-facing slopes: Shortleaf pine (30%), Post oak, Blackjack oak, Black oak, Black hickory.

Ridgetop: White oak, Blackjack oak, Post oak, Black hickory.

Some of the species that cannot survive a clearcut are Ginseng, Strawberry bush, Beech drops, Showy orchid, Partridgeberry, pawpaw, Sugar huckleberry, American beech, Bitternut hickory, Ozark chinkapin, Carolina basswood, and the endangered Rich Mountain goldenrod and Rich Mountain salamander.

In 1986, the Forest Service issued its final Land and Resource Management Plan to continue the foregoing destructive practices for the next fifty years.

Arkansas and Oklahoma (and one Texas) environmental organizations have appealed from that plan to the Chief of the Forest Service. Their primary grounds are clearcutting and desecration of natural diversity. Among the appellants are:

Oklahoma Wilderness Coalition, Oklahoma Chapter of the Sierra Club, Arkansas Chapter of the Sierra Club, Oklahoma Wildlife Federation, The Wilderness Society, LeFlore County Wilderness Association, Texas Committee on Natural Resources, Oklahoma Wild Turkey Federation, Scenic Rivers Association of Oklahoma, Mike Crawford, and the Arkansas Conservation Coalition.

Senator Dale Bumpers, of Arkansas, has written a letter to the Supervisor of the National Forest criticizing the plan.

The citizen groups include at least two trial lawyers in their numbers, Mike Crawford and Jim Stanley. Mike, in particular, has not concealed his conception that citizens may file court action if the Ouachita Plan is not revised by replacing most of the even-age management with selection management.

To avoid, or at least defer, a lawsuit, the Ouachita Supervisor, Mike Curran, has withdrawn the Forest Plan for revision. Curran told a Pow Wow of clearcutting opponents from many states on May 7, 1988, that "clearcutting in the Ouachita is on its way out." Unfortunately, it is a very slow departure. The FY 1988 schedule called for 15,000 acres of even-age logging and only 1,500 acres of experimental selection plots.

In September of 1988, the Ouachita chief planner revealed tentatively that under a Supplemental Plan 100,000 acres of timberland, already required to be removed from clearcuts, would be managed under even-age or selection, whichever each multi-disciplinary team decided when preparing prescriptions for various compartments, from time to time. That is the way it has supposedly been done in the past, but the teams always decided upon even-age.

The Supplemental Plan, due in April 1989, provides hope for more selection management in the 900,000 acres, but leaves little leeway to file a lawsuit until each individual site-specific prescription is made, scattered through the years to come. The Forest Service is attempting to make it impossible to maintain a lawsuit against a forest-wide program.

In state after state, the agency is employing similar delay strategies, as will be shown in the final chapter.

A tough confluence of loggers, hunters, local business folk, and environmentalists got together with local Congressman Wes Watkins in Southeastern Oklahoma and by-passed the entire clearcutting hierarchy.

John Dennington, President of the Southeast Oklahoma Sportsmen's Association, Noel Bethel, a selection logger, and Audrey Ballentine, who formed a LeFlore County Wilderness Association, called a little meeting to discuss what to do about all the clearcutting. Everybody around Poteau wanted to come, but the room was too small. They got Weyerhauser's agreement not to clearcut all the way to the creeks on its vast properties. But the Forest Service was adamant. So they called another meeting in a school auditorium.

This time, 700 people came, including John Wilson, representing the Poteau Chamber of Commerce. They soon got the attention of Congressman Watkins. Ballentine had been trying for years to interest Watkins in sponsoring some wildernesses as a way to stop clearcutting. So had some Sierra Club members from places like Tulsa and Oklahoma City. This time, by good fortune, Beth Johnson had become regional representative for the Southern Plains Region. Out of that confluence of minds and spirits emerged an ambitious plan.

The Congressman would file a bill designating thousands of acres of Ouachita NF as wilderness, thousands more as scenic areas, and even larger areas as a Winding Stair Mountain National Recreation Area and Indian Nations National Scenic and Wildlife Area, where timber harvesting would be prohibited along the Talimena Scenic Highway, and restricted to the selection system as far as users of that highway could see. The plan even called for maintenance of natural diversity, with hardwoods particularly in mind. No more pine plantations in the national recreation area.

They got Oklahoma Senators David Boren and Don Nickles to join in the concept. Bills were filed in both houses of Congress. The Forest Service fought them. Facing defeat, the agency lobbyists whittled away at the language. They tried to create loopholes in the definitions of selection management and diversity. Years before, they had perverted the selective harvesting language in the Hell's Canyon NRA. But this time up in Washington, D.C., Beth Johnson insisted on retaining strong language. She succeeded fairly well.

The final bill protects 97,346 acres from clearcutting, an ingenious precedent for potential forest reforms in other national forests across the land.

THE TEXAS DESECRATION

The May 1987, Forest Service Plan calls for clearcutting sixty percent of the available commercial timber in the four national forests of Texas and sccd-trcc or shelterwood cutting the rest. That totals 521,000 acres.

They had already clearcut about thirty percent of that total since 1964.

See Color Plate 11.

The Forest Service has labeled ninety-four percent of the available timber as pine sites, presuming that pines can be cultivated into dominance there, no matter what was the composition of trees before human interference. Some experts, including their own vegetation mapper, A. W. Kuechler, have found that the vegetation that would exist today if humans were removed from the scene would be mainly oak/hickory/pine, beech/magnolia/loblolly, and southern floodplain forest, all dominated by hardwoods. Originally, there were probably about 10,000 to 15,000 acres of Longleaf pine/scrub oak upland parklands included.

The Forest Service claims that it would allow thirty percent of the canopy of its pine stands to be hardwoods. Even this much would be impossible under the hardwood suppression measures that the agency is applying and intends to continue.

Those measures are as follows.

After marking, advertising, and selling the pines and sometimes a number of hardwoods in a "pine" stand of seven to fifty acres, and after the purchaser saws down the marked trees, the Forest Service hires employees or a contractor to enter the shambles with heavy equipment, knock down the remaining trees and vegetation, and push it into windrows or chop it.

They then plant pine seedlings, mostly Loblollies. In about three years, dewberries, greenbriars, and broom sedge tangle with the pines.

On occasion they use herbicides and pesticides to kill plants that compete with and insects that eat the young pines.

In about twenty years, when the pines grow tall enough to survive a ground fire, the Forest Service conducts a low burn, deadening the oak, hickory, and gum sprouts and everything else that has sprung up from whatever roots and seeds survived all the bulldozing. They even burn some of the young pines, but they had planted them densely enough to need thinning, anyway.

Every three to five years, when sprouts come up again, the Forest Service burns again, and again, until the stand is as completely pine as they can get it. If any other trees manage to survive the burning, the Forest Service often turns crews loose to girdle, to cut, or to poison them. They call this "timber stand improvement."

After about thirty or forty years, the Forest Service advertises for a commercial thinning. Timber operators bid. The highest bidder cuts and sells pines marked for thinning. This may happen repeatedly.

Finally, the stand reaches rotation age (seventy years for loblolly pines, eighty for shortleaf and longleaf pines. The Forest Service marks the merchantable pines and sells them to the highest (sometimes the only) bidder, who cuts them all, mangling most of the unmarked trees. The process then starts all over again.

So much for the "pine" stands. The six percent of the stands that even the Forest Service acknowledges as hardwood sites fare little better. But here, after the clearcut and site preparation, the Forest Service does not plant pines. The roots and stumps sprout into what the bureaucrats describe as "vigorous young shoots," from two to thirty-five of them to a former tree. Numerous pines also spring up from seeds, because site preparation lays the field bare for a year or so, and pine trees are always nearby. The result is a mixed forest too dense for high-level production of hardwood timber.

Since pervasive clearcutting began in 1964, these hardwood "regenerations" are not old enough for commercial thinnings. We do not yet know what the Forest Service will do with them. We have reason to suspect that wherever the pines are big enough, the Forest Service will tend to thin away the oaks, gums, and hickories around them, thus utilizing even "hardwood" sites for growing as many pine sawlogs as possible by the next clearcutting time.

Private companies, including Temple-Eastex and Champion International, have been engaged in a similar practice, except that they usually burn their windrows and clearcut larger areas.

Louisiana-Pacific is doing selection management on a million acres across the South, including Texas. For reasons of cost efficiency, Temple-Eastex has retained a few of its selection stands along roadways as demonstration areas.

As a result of erosion from wholesale clearcuts, sand has piled up in most streambeds. Branches that formerly flowed year-round have become intermittent or dry. In rainy spells, the areas flood worse, but in droughts, when people need water the most, the streams do not supply as much water as before all the clearcutting.

The clearcutting process has reduced the beech/magnolia forest type to a precious few hundred acres, almost entirely within two wildernesses and two scenic areas in the national forests and a few preserves outside. That type is now designated as threatened in Texas. *See drawing, "Lullaby of the Pines," page 115.*

Also threatened is the Longleaf pine/tallgrass community, because Longleaf pines do not transplant well after a clearcut. Frequent prescribed burning is gradually wiping out the Bluejack, Blackjack, and Southern red oaks from under the Longleaf pines that survive. The oak/hickory/pine community never comes back in a pine plantation. So much for the major forest types that formerly dominated East Texas. It used to be called "The Pineywoods" because east of the mountains, East Texas is about the only part of the state where pines grew at all. Now, it is becoming the region where pines are dominant everywhere from stream to upland. And even where Longleaf and Shortleaf pines once dominated, the foresters are now raising Loblollies.

All this clearcutting has eliminated many species of trees and other plants from each area cut. In the entire clearcutting spree since it began in 1964, no beech, beech drops, nor cranefly orchids have returned. Shagbark, Nutmeg, and Black hickory, Black walnut and Florida maple have not returned. It is doubtful if they ever will. Basswood and Southern magnolia do not return for twenty years, and then slowly, if at all. Attached is a list of shade-loving late succession smaller species that have not returned to the areas clearcut, and may never do so.

See Table III.

Unlike the Forest Service, a number of private timber opera-tors do not clearcut in some or all of their stands. Louisiana-Pacific practices uneven-age multi-species management on its stands in Texas and elsewhere, about one million acres. It also prefers the se-lection system on 200,000 acres of other owners that it manages. Gibbs Brothers manages 55,000 acres under the selection system. Many smaller operators use single-tree selection, although the Texas Forest Service, a state agency, advises most small operators to clearcut and raise pines.

The Attorney General of Texas and several citizen groups, in-cluding the Sierra Club and Texas Committee on Natural Re-sources, have made administrative appeals from the final Plan and EIS for the National Forests in Texas. Their principle grounds are against wholesale clearcutting and for native diversity. They expect they will have to appeal the Chief's final ruling to court.

The Forest Service Regional Forester in Atlanta has invited the public to suggest issues for a region-wide environmental impact statement on vegetation management in the South. He listed the following measures: mechanical equipment, hand tools, herbicides, prescribed burning, and combinations of these. Citizen groups are suggesting the alternatives of single-tree selection with all-age all-species native diversity, but the Regional Forester has replied that such broad management policy is beyond the scope of his EIS.

Unless the Forest Service makes an unexpected about-face, the only lasting remedy would come through strengthening of the Na-tional Forest Management Act by Congress.

THEY ARE EVEN-AGING THE WILD SAN JUAN

If you walk far enough northward up a clear cool stream near the southern boundary of the San Juan National Forest, through foothills bedecked with Pinon pine and Western juniper, you will begin to inhale that cool, sprucy fragrance of Ponderosa pine, Blue spruce, and Gambel oak, and you will begin to see clearcuts man-aged mainly for pine.

Still higher and cooler, you can observe the realm of Engel-

TABLE III.

SOME FORBS AND SHRUBS THAT CLEARCUTTING ELIMINATES FROM THE SITE IN TEXAS

Latin Name	Common Name
Botrychium dissectum	Cutleaf grapefern
Asplenium platyneuron	Ebony spleenwort
Athyrium felix-femina	Lady fern
Onoclea sensibilis	Sensitive fern
Polypodium polypodioides	Resurrection fern
Thelypteris kunthii	Shield fern
Aira caryophyllea	Silver haregrass
Chasmanthium laxum	Smooth sheathed spikegrass
Chasmanthium sessiliflorum	Short-stalked spikegrass
Dicanthelium ravenelii	Broad leaved dicanthelium
Panicum anceps	Panicum anceps
Carex blanda	Bent lip sedge
Carex amphibola	Amphibious sedge
Carex cephalophora	Woodbank sedge
Carex frankii	Frank's sedge
Carex retroflexa	Reflexed sedge
Scerlia oligantha	Littlehead nutrush
Arisaema dracontium	Green dragon
Arisaema triphyllum	Jack in the pulpit
Polygonatum biflorum	Solomon's seal
Trillium gracile	Graceful trillium
Corallorhiza wisteriana	Coralroot orchid
Tipularia discolor	Crippled cranefly orchid
Aristolochia tomentosa	Wooly pipevine
Xanthorhiza simplicissima	Yellowroot
Sanguinaria canadensis	Bloodroot
Hydrangea quercifolia	Oakleaf hydrangea
Itea virginica	Sweetspire
Hamamelis virginiana	Witch hazel
Agrimonia rostellata	Agrimony
Desmodium rotundifolium	Prostrate tick clover
Desmodium nudiflorum	Bare stemmed tick clover
Euonymus americanus	Strawberry bush
Berchemia scandens	Supplejack
Stewartia malacodendron	Silky camellia
Passiflora lutea	Yellow passion flower
Sanicula canadensis	Snakeroot
Rhododendron oblongifolia	White azalea
Rhododendron prinophyllum	Azalea
Halesia diptera	*Silverbell*
Chionanthus virginica	Fringe free
Bartonia texana	Bartonia
Perilla frutescens	Beefsteak plant
Dicliptera brachiata	False mint
Viburnum dentatum	*Arrowwood viburnum*
Lobelia cardinalis	Cardinal flower

mann spruce and Subalpine fir, and can see more clearcuts scattered along the mountainsides, coming back to spruce.

Along the streams and rockslides, and in old burn-outs up the steeper slopes, you will notice the light green vigor of Quaking aspens, and will see where patches of them, too, have been clearcut.

At all elevations between the foothills and the timberline in this mountain paradise lost, you will see clearcuts.

The 1987 amendment to the 1983 Plan for the San Juan calls for even-age management of all the available commercial timber for the next decade, as follows:

Clearcut	9939 acres
Shelterwood seed	6612 acres
"Selection"	2523 acres

The "selection" cuts are mainly or altogether one to three acres in size, too large to conform with the definition of selection management by anyone except a bureaucrat.

In addition, the schedule includes 15,783 acres of shelterwood site preparation by "Tractor" (bulldozer), auguring a great flood of this two-and three-stage form of clearcutting and ground disturbing in the following decade.

Hopes for salvation of the San Juan lie in its vast wildernesses, the Weimenuche, the Lizard Head, and the South San Juan. Rising to 14,000-foot peaks they cover about 600,000 acres. About half of the wilderness land is too low or high to produce commercial timber. Altogether, the national forest contains 1.9 million acres. Subtract the wildernesses, some other protected or developed areas, and the non-forested areas, and we have 470,000 acres of available commercial timber, a majority of which is mature and has never been harvested.

In its environmental impact statement, the Forest Service characterizes this great forest cloak as "overmature," with "low vigor" and "high mortality" and limited wildlife diversity. It says that the aspen stands are dying and will not regenerate unless harvested or burned.

Citizen groups conducted a long, hard challenge to the San Juan Plan and EIS, based mainly on its recreational shortcomings. The Forest Service re-worked its recreational documentations and reduced its timber sale volume (as in above ten-year figures), but retained its even-age management level at one hundred percent of the available commercial timber, unless the supervisor includes some individual-tree selection in the nine percent designation "selection."

In their appeal from the 1983 Plan, Natural Resources Defense Council and other groups presented scientific evidence that the San Juan is "an outstanding but fragile natural resource," mainly with "good to excellent inherent vegetative diversity," losing only 0.5% of its volume annually to mortality, offset by new growth of four times that amount.

Two independent forest economists calculated that at least 3/4 of the areas slated for timber management would lose money on the planned timber program. NRDC argued that such lands should be removed from the timber base and preserved for recreation and watershed protection. Clearcutting, said NRDC, causes the worst visual harms of all logging, and causes excessive sedimentation that hampers fish propagation and kills natural stream vegetation, decreasing fish populations.

Where a fourth of the total land in a region will be clearcut, the impact is less apparent than in smaller, flatter forests, as in Texas, that face clearcutting in a far higher percentage of their total land. The San Juan region, as a whole, will be less fragmented. Furthermore, most visitors will go to the wildernesses and will never see the clearcuts.

Yet, clearcutting, if it proceeds, would severely impact almost half a million acres. And these acres form a great interconnected biogeographical island along the southern slopes of the San Juan Mountains, well below the Continental Divide, which runs easterly and westerly here.

All this clearcutting would also erode the slopes that are vital to future timber production and wildlife preservation, and erode the excellent trout streams that flow southward from the San Juan Range, including those that I have fished since my youth.

If there were no alternative method, this area might be among the least harmful to be clearcut. But there is the alternative of selection management, which would essentially spare the biogeographical integrity of this half-million acres.

For generations, the Forest Service practiced the basics of selection forestry by thinning stands for sawlogs and poles. This practice could and should resume, bolstered by the complete long-range principles of selection management. In that way, the residents and tourists of the area, including Durango, Pagosa Springs, and the people of Southern Ute Indian Reservation, may continue to enjoy to the full the multiple-use benefits of the resplendent San Juan.

WASHINGTON: A CAMEO OF NORTHWEST FORESTS

Washington is suffering the destruction of its natural forests by a four-sided onslaught. The Forest Service, U.S. Bureau of Indian Affairs, and state agencies are clearcutting massively. So are private landowners.

They are logging every steepness of timbered slopes, even eighty-degree inclines. The Forest Service does not mark the trees' to be cut but merely tags the boundaries and lets the buyers take everything they desire. On the steepest concave slopes, they are sky-lining the logs to loading platforms so as to prevent ripping up the ground, but erosion is still heavy. On lesser slopes, they are high-leading the logs so that only one end drags. The Forest Service has generally burned the residue. The other agencies drag the slash and stumps into piles and let them rot. Every variation of method leaves a barren, eroding landscape.

From the high Cascades westward, the managers are clearcutting mixed forests and planting Douglasfir. As a result, the natural communities are disappearing: Douglasfir/Western hemlock/Western redcedar/Sitka spruce at lower elevations; Douglasfir/silver fir/western hemlock at higher elevations; and Mountain hemlock/Noble fir/Silver fir/Douglasfir at high elevations, all with rich diversity of sub-canopy and ground vegetation. On some south-facing slopes where the sunlight is too harsh even for young Douglasfirs, the managers substitute shelterwood cutting for clearcutting.

Western Oregon is facing a similar picture, as in Mt. Hood National Forest.

See photo "Clobbered."

Further east in Washington, they are clearcutting mixed communities and planting ponderosa pine on lower elevations and letting lodgepole pine revegetate at higher elevations.

They have decimated the mature stands of 200- to 1000-year-old monsters, up to twenty-five feet in circumference. Only one million acres of old-growth remains, almost entirely in the national forests. The new management plans of the Forest Service call for clearcutting all the remaining available commercial timber in the

"Clobbered," Mt. Hood National Forest, Oregon (northwestern), 1988. By Peter Stewartt.

The Forest Service has desecrated this region more totally than any air force has ever blanketed an area of similar size. More than sixty large clearcuts fragment the habitat to the point of extinction of many species and exclusion of most human visitors. To get the picture you have to fly above it, which is what Project Lighthawk did here for the national media.

national forests, except for a strictly limited number of species indicator habitats, mainly for spotted owls.

The Bureau of Indian Affairs manages about 500,000 acres of
timberland in western Washington. Its bureaucrats have sold timber on thirty-year contracts, at give-away prices, as low as five dollars per thousand board feet, all being clearcut. About 50,000 acres
of that are the remnants of old-growth not yet cut.

The state department of natural resources is managing a million acres of public school timber lands and one million acres of
other state timber mainly for clearcut sales.

Except for three national parks and many scattered camp-
grounds, recreation areas, and special areas, the three government
agencies have already gone halfway along a course of eliminating
the natural diversity of Washington's forests. On the Olympic Pen-
insula, they have already cut so heavily around Olympic National
Park that it sticks up like an oasis in the desert. Intentionally or
not, the agencies have assured that the national park can never be
expanded so as to link up with any other old-growth stands and
thereby to reduce the ongoing fragmentation.

In all this process, the clearcutters are endangering those animals and plants which require shady old forests for survival. They
include the spotted owl and red vole. A blue ribbon panel of the
National Audubon Society has estimated that only 2,000 pairs of
spotted owls remain in the Pacific Northwest. The Forest Service
plans to manage 550 scattered habitats of 2,200 acres each for spotted owl. Many of these selected spotted owl management acres are
unoccupied and vulnerable to being removed from protection. The
Washington State Game Department has found that the minimum
viable habitat of the species is 4,500 acres per pair.

Washington environmentalists have attacked the Forest Service draft environmental impact statement on spotted owls, and are
protesting the management plans in each forest as they come out.
Principal complaints are the destruction of old-growth and the ad-
herence to a seventy- to one hundred-year rotation basis, far too
short for old-growth ever to return.

Seattle Audubon Society has extended its protest all the way to
some individual groves, including the "Fly Area" on the upper
North Fork of the Snoqualmie River, where the spotted owl has
been seen. Here, Audubon leaders insisted on an adequate environmental assessment before the Forest Service could sell the thou-

sand-year-old stands. Audubon extracted a promise from the Forest Service to notify them before any timber sales. The bureaucrats evaded this promise by making a so-called "salvage" sale where some trees had blown down. More than half the trees "salvaged" had survived the storm, including Douglasfirs up to twenty-five feet in circumference, but the "salvage" operation removed everything, leaving a broad gash in the old-growth. In the process, the Forest Service lengthened a spur road into the remaining forest. Audubon conservation committee members Tom Campion and Rick Rutz state that the Forest Service is determined to fragment the spotted owl habitat, if for no other reason than to show who controls the forest. Campion and Rutz cite many other examples of Forest Service chicanery.

A STRATEGY OF DELAY

When on weak grounds stall. That is the strategy of the Forest Service as to clearcutting. When first confronted, the bureaucracy stands firm. When threatened with a lawsuit, it delays. While delaying, it usually offers to concede something. The magnitude of its concession is proportional to the imminence of the threat.

In the chapter on Virginia and Oklahoma/Arkansas, the Forest Service agreed to present, in 1989, a goal of how many acres should be converted to selection management, but insisted in deferring decisions on locations for such management until time to make a site-specific prescription. The Supervisor of the Ouachaita National Forest has postponed issuing even the Supplemental Plan three times, while merrily clearcutting all the way.

In the Texas lawsuit, the Forest Service is using the "site-specific" tactic as a major defense. In 1987, after taking eleven years, the agency produced a management plan that still embraced one hundred percent even-age management, almost the same as before. When TCONR, Sierra, and others filed administrative appeals the agency indicated it would need at least two years to rule in them. TCONR and Sierra requested that the agency defer all, or many, clearcut sales in the interim, so that the very forests that the appeals were trying to protect would not be ripped up during the long appeal. F. Dale Robertson, Chief of the Forest Service, denied that request for the single reason that such a stay would hurt the timber industry and the economy.

Robertson added that his ruling would not harm the citizens

because they could, in the meanwhile, file appeals against individual sale proposals, and the agency would consider them on a site-specific basis.

For two years, this ruling destroyed any opportunity that the citizens had to challenge the entire one hundred percent even-age program. The agency thereby limited citizen suits to tiny bites at the apple, strung out over a long period of time.

The Chief's Fabian tactic has thus far succeeded. When TCONR added to its lawsuit a claim for preliminary injunction against clearcut sales until the Forest Service ruled on TCONR's entire administrative appeal, Judge Robert M. Parker denied this claim.

TCONR proceeded to file requests for stays of individual clearcut sale proposals, as they were offered, but the Forest Service dismissed these requests as untimely, on the theory that the clearcutting had been decided upon years earlier, when prescriptions were made under the old system. TCONR argued that the Forest Service had not provided TCONR any notice of those prescriptions so that they could be challenged at the time of decision. The Forest Service replied that every year it sent an advance schedule of proposed timber sales, and TCONR could have appealed after the first such notice. TCONR responded that such schedule did not provide any vital details, such as whether a sale involved clearcutting or mere thinning. Also, TCONR pointed out that the Forest Service changes its prescriptions and annual schedules frequently, therefore they are not final decisions that trigger the appeal deadline. The agency rejected this argument.

So, in Texas, the agency has thus far used its site-specific ploy effectively.

On August 31, 1988, in his decision on the Flathead National Forest in Montana, the Chief broadened his site-specific defense to cover just about every substantive program in a forest plan. In the appeal by Swan View Coalition, Resources Unlimited, and Five Valleys Audubon Society, the Chief held that a forest plan does not prescribe "specific management direction." He opined that the National Forest Management Act intended to establish a "dynamic management system" for "integrated consideration" of various factors in undertaking future actions. He assured that the agency will make further analysis prior to undertaking a specific management activities.

The Chief upheld his Regional Forester's findings that clearcutting is the optimum method in most of the forest, but cleverly stated that this finding does not constitute a final decision. Site-specific determinations will be made later!

If the Chief's opinion of Congressional intent in NFMA holds up, it would be virtually impossible to win a lawsuit against a program, like pervasive clearcutting, set forth in a forest plan. Citizens would have to bring lawsuit after lawsuit, on site after site, and prove that each proposed clearcut, or seed-tree, or shelterwood cut is not optimum or not appropriate. Since every site varies somewhat from all others, no court decision would provide a binding precedent for future cases.

Very few, if any, citizen groups have the resources to bring enough site-specific lawsuits to make a substantial dent in pervasive clearcutting.

Even though the site-specific tactic is a diabolical method for an agency to suppress citizen participation in reform, there is a serious danger the Forest Service will get away with it in many courts. In every lawsuit where a citizen group seeks a ruling on an entire program, as in the Texas case, the Forest Service will plead that the court should not hear it, because the citizens should wait until a site-specific decision arises, and should file an administrative appeal on that specific decision before going to court. After all, the Forest Service might grant the appeal, so the court would never have to hear the case.

That kind of argument is always attractive to a federal judge, because every one of them is overworked. Whatever can be left to an agency means that much less effort for the courts.

Congress could solve the problem by amending NFMA to state clearly that any programmatic decision in a forest plan, especially any decision on the extent of even-age management or clearcutting, is ripe for judicial review.

In addition to NFMA and the Endangered Species Act another legal tool for challenging a forest plan is the National Environmental Policy Act. But NEPA goes only to the procedures of decision-making. If an agency follows the prescribed procedures, and genuinely considers key environmental impacts, you cannot use NEPA to cancel its decision.

The Forest Service knows this well. In the Flathead decision, the Chief directed the Regional Forester to clarify the portions of the environmental impact statement that describe existing and projected old growth habitat.

In order to delay lawsuits, the Forest Service is adept at with-drawing, supplementing, or amending environmental impact statements. It can extend that process for years.

In summary, the Forest Service continuously utilizes loopholes to frustrate enforcement of existing laws covering forest practices, loopholes that Forest Service lobbyists like former Chief Max Peterson worked into the legislation before passage. The only solution is to get Congress to strengthen the laws, eliminating the loopholes.

SELECTION FORESTS ARE A TREAT FOR SORE EYES

We toured the southland to see the trees; and what did we see? We saw the pits.

We saw clearcuts and so-called wildlife cuts. We saw seed-tree cuts and shelterwood cuts. And they were all far worse than they were cracked up to be.

While flying across the Jefferson National Forest in Virginia, we saw twenty-six recent clearcuts in two square miles.

We walked through new clearcuts in Cherokee National Forest, Tennessee, that loomed high over the Conesauga River, a proposed wild and scenic river. Nearby, we saw the boundary marks of a scheduled clearcut sale on a steep slope above a creek that runs into that river less than a mile away. These and other clearcuts threaten the fabled clearness of the Conesauga.

In the Chattahoochee National Forest in Georgia, we saw chocolate-colored water flowing into a clear creek from a new road. One timber purchaser had pushed the road along the bank of the creek in order to haul logs from a clearcut then taking place.

Clearcutting means felling virtually all the trees in a stand. If completed in a period of three to twenty years, foresters refer to it as a seed-tree or shelterwood cut. A system aimed toward one or more of these cutting methods is called even-age management. We call it all "clearcutting."

In all ten national forests that we visited on the ground, and the other six that we saw from our plane, the Forest Service is using clearcutting as the principal harvest method, and even-age management as the system.

But, we also saw, like a rainbow, some beautiful, private forests in Alabama, Georgia, Indiana, Illinois, and Missouri. These forests are thriving under the individual tree selection system, where the owner periodically sells some of the older trees and some of the youngest trees that are too dense, leaving the large majority to grow on until future harvests.

We saw such stands in hardwood bottomlands, mixed hardwood and loblolly slopes, Longleaf pine upland grasslands, Shortleaf pine and hardwood uplands, and oak-hickory mountainsides. Natural regeneration is producing young trees of all ages and all species, contrary to Forest Service claims that clearcutting is necessary to obtain regeneration.

In these selection forests, the soil and leaf litter were rich and thick under our feet. A wide diversity of herbs and shrubs, from blueberries to Mountain laurel were growing lushly.

Narrow roads traversed these woods under the shade of the tall trees, contrasting with the wide, open, heavily constructed roads in national forest harvesting areas.

Unlike national forests in the eastern mountains, these selection forests are all bringing in a return greater than their costs. For example, Wilmon Timberlands, in the rugged hills of southwestern Alabama, saves not only the expenses of site preparation and planting, but also the huge costs that the Forest Service expends on killing hardwoods by girdling and poisoning ("timber stand improvement") and by prescribed burning. Wilmon raises trees of many species, including Longleaf pines, with very little hardwood pruning and no burning. In selection forests, the stronger young trees thin out the weaklings naturally by outgrowing them.

In derogation of Forest Service claims that selection management requires a greater density of permanent roads than even-age management, Wilmon has no more roads per square mile than national forest timberland in the same region, and fewer permanent roads. Furthermore, Wilmon's smaller roads do not cause as much erosion.

Wilmon has a great variety and density of wildlife, including the rare Red-hills box turtle. We saw and heard far more birds there than on any national forest we visited. Wilmon makes a side profit from leasing to deer and turkey hunters.

The Forest Service sent a batch of its officials to visit Wilmon years ago, but has not reported its findings, nor any of the foregoing facts, in the 125 draft and 66 final environmental impact statements that it has issued. These statements describe selection (they call it "uneven-age") management in a totally different light than we observed.

See photo "Natural Stand Management."

"Natural Stand Management," Alabama, 1987.
    This White oak/Loblolly pine stand on Wilmon Timberlands illustrates how
pleasant it can be to gaze upon forest that is managed by improvement cuts — careful
removal of the trees of lower quality, leaving the best of all sizes and species.

Selection management addresses each site, and actually each tree, individually. Yet it is feasible in operations as large as national forests. With only four foresters, Wilmon manages 51,000 acres. Leon Neel, in southern Georgia, manages 73,000 acres with only two full-time foresters. Leo Drey, in southeastern Missouri, has 153,000 acres in selection forestry.

Selection management is also appropriate for small holdings. In southern Indiana, a Bedford jeweler and his wife do most of the work on weekends on their 400-acre hardwood/pine forest. A state forester showed them how to do it, and suggested some reference books. In southern Illinois, Tommy Thompson does all the thinning and marking for harvest on his 140-acre hardwood stand during hours when he is not on his regular job in town.

We were delighted to find that many in these areas not only oppose wholesale clearcutting, a universal sentiment, but also understand the values of single-tree selection as the widely favored alternative. Practically nobody we met accepts the Forest Service's criticisms of selection harvesting.

In Virginia, Dr. Leon Minckler showed us another alternative to even-age management: group selection. A former researcher for the Forest Service, Dr. Minckler has written texts on the subject. The Ranger of the Blacksburg District in Jefferson National Forest has authorized Dr. Minckler to mark and to monitor a five-acre group selection stand. The openings range up to about one-third acre. Oaks, tulip trees, and other hardwoods are regenerating successfully only a year after a cut. The soil and most of the leaf litter are intact. Forest Service employees used rakes to expose the soil in places for seedlings to sprout better. More natural diversity survives there than in a clearcut or a nearby shelterwood cut, but less than in the single-tree selection stands that we had seen.

Although group selection is better than even-age management, it is difficult to define in a few words. I would not want to leave it open for Forest Service personnel to use group selection at their discretion because they are too adept at taking advantage of shades of definition. They would probably wind up with a conglomeration of small clearcuts, instead of a single-tree group selection system.

The practice of both selection systems (group and individual tree) maintains stands of all ages and preserves natural diversity from soil to top of canopy. Clearcutting results in one-age stands or, in the case of very small clearcuts, stands of one-age clumps, with minimal regard for natural diversity.

For advocates of occasional group selection harvests, a restriction to single-tree selection will not preclude occasional harvests of small groups. It would still be possible to cut several trees in a clump, on occasions where the cutting of individual trees would not open up enough sunlight for regeneration of some shade-intolerant species that are needed, like Loblolly or Longleaf pine. We saw some spots where Leon Neel had done that in individual-tree selection stands.

If you're wondering who "we" are, Charles "Lighthawk" Jamieson was our smooth pilot and Brad Moore was our photographer on the grueling fifteen-day flying tour.

Here are the national forests that we visited on the ground, all loaded with clearcuts: Delta in Mississippi; Apalachicola in Florida; Chattahoochee in Georgia; Cherokee in Tennessee; Jefferson in Virginia; George Washington in Virginia; Monongahela in West Virginia; Hoosier in Indiana; Shawneee in Illinois; and Mark Twain in Missouri.

In most of them, we got tired of clearcuts and also visited a beautiful wilderness or scenic area. But perhaps our greatest thrill came from meeting people who have struggled for years, like us, in an effort to talk the Forest Service into responsible forestry but have arrived at the same conclusion that we have. As in sociology, I call this process convergence. We have converged on the conviction that only congressional action will lead the Forest Service to restrain its clearcutting.

Many people have come to think alike about clearcutting. They range from young out-of-work writers living on farms to mature well-to-do foresters. With two exceptions, anybody with intelligence who repeatedly sees how much the Forest Service is clearcutting becomes an ardent opponent of the Forest Service. The exceptions are higher-ups in the Forest Service or certain timber purchasers who depend on Forest Service timber.

SELECTION FORESTS YOU CAN SEE ON REQUEST

INTRODUCTION

Although selection management is the classic silvicultural system, federal agencies practice it on only a tiny fraction of the 100 million acres of federal lands where logging takes place. Instead, on practically all federal forests, the agencies are using even-age management. This means clearcutting and its two- or three-stage variations.

Even-age management is extremely severe, replacing the existing forest with a a new stand of commercial trees, generally of only one species. It vastly reduces native diversity, drastically curtails most forms of outdoor recreation, depletes the soil, and impairs water quality.

Selection management, where properly practiced is far superior in every respect. It is also more cost-efficient.

Although many private enterprises, large and small, practice selection management, most citizens have never seen it. Once people see it, they enthusiastically support it in place of pervasive even-age logging.

To give people a chance to see selection forests, here is a list of some of them. We would welcome whatever additions you may offer.

SELECTION FORESTS LIST

State	Location and Acreage	Contact and Phone	Address
AL	S. Central 51,000	Wilmon Timberland, Frank Stewart, Jr. (205) 337-4417	P.O. Box 165 Vredenberg, AL 36481
AR	Central 176,000 and S. Central 200,000	Deltic Farm and Properties Louis Rainey (501) 862-6411	200 Peach St. El Dorado, AR 71730
CA	Northeast 87,000	Collins Pine Carl Murray (916) 258-2111	P.O. Box 796 Chester, CA 96020
FL	Northwest	Tall Timbers Research Sta. (904) 893-4153	Tallahassee, FL 32301
GA	South 73,000 (Wade Tract, etc)	Leon Neel Consultant (912) 226-8432	P.O. Box 1043 Thomasville, GA 31799
IL	South 40	Tom Thompson	c/o Ace, Rt. 1 Brookport, IL 62910
IN	South	Dr. Leon Toliver (812) 936-4616	122 Maple St./ French Lick, IN 47432
MO	Southeast 153,000	Pioneer Forest Leon Drey (314) 241-7762 Clinton Trammell	515 West Point/St. Louis, MO 63130 / P.O. Box 497/Salem, MO 65560
NH	500,000	Society for the Protection of New Hampshire Forests, Paul O. Bofinger (603) 224-9935	54 Portsmouth St. Concord, NH 03301
NC	West 150	Walton R. Smith (704) 524-3186	221 Huckleberry Cr. Rd. Franklin, NC 28734

OR	Southwest	Dick Chasm (503) 679-7560	P.O. Box 51 Dillard, OR 97432
OR	North 5,000	Individual Tree Selection Mgt. Scott Ferguson (503) 222-9772	American Bank Bldg. Suite 204 Portland, OR 97205
TX	Southeast 55,000	Gibbs Brothers W. L. Carroll (409) 295-9371	First Ntl Bank Bldg./ Huntsville, TX 77340
VT	?? 500,000	Forest Resource Services John McClain (802) 728-3742	Main Street Randolph, VT 05060
VA	Southwest 5	Dr. Leon Minckler (705) 951-1108	623 Bogie Ln. Rt. 4, Country Club Estates/ Blacksburg, VA 24060
WI	Northwest 400	Charles H. Stoddard (715) 466-2480	Rt. 2, Box 83 Minong, WI 54859

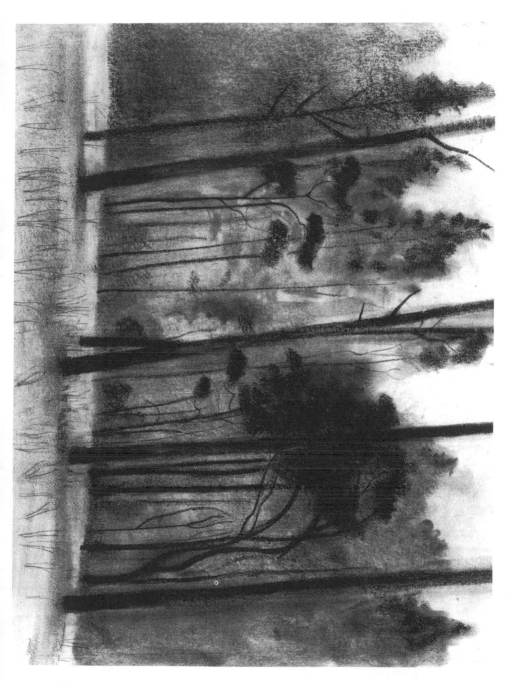

"Lullaby of the Pines," Angelina NF, Texas (southeastern), 1988. Drawing by Anne Weary.

Glossary

Clearcutting: Strictly from a forester's definition, the logging of all commercial trees in a patch or stand in a short period of time.

In this book, as in many localities, the term is used broadly to include the variations called seed-tree and shelterwood, and to include follow-up leveling of vegetation that survives the clearcut (see "Site preparation," below), seeding or planting of new trees of the species desired, and burning, poisoning, cutting, or otherwise reducing species other than the species seeded or planted.

Cutting cycle: The planned, recurring lapse of time between successive loggings in a timber stand.

Even-age Management: The growing of commercial timber so that all trees in a stand are generally within five years of the same age. The stand is logged completely by clearcutting, seed-tree cutting or shelterwood cutting. Then the site is "prepared." A new stand of commercial species is started. "Undesirable" species are periodically "suppressed." Commercial species are usually thinned a time or two. At end of rotation, another total cut follows.

Midstory: The tier of trees in the middle range of height in a stand.

Native diversity: The same or similar composition of living species in the same or similar relative densities and dominance as would inhabit each stand in the same period of time, in the absence of substantial human impact.

Regeneration: The commencement of a new tree or stand in a forest. When the Forest Service says, "regeneration cut" it means only an even-age cut, in spite of the fact that selection harvests are also followed by regeneration.

Reserve tree: A tree designated to be left in a clearcut for a reason such as wildlife habitat.

Rotation: The planned number of years between the commencement of a stand of trees and its final cutting at a specified stage of growth. This term applies only to even-age stands.

Seed tree: A tree not removed in the first stage of an even-age cut in order to drop seeds to generate a new crop.

Seed tree cut: A logging operation that leaves one or more seed trees, generally 6 to 10 per acre.

117

Seed tree removal: The subsequent entry into a seed tree or shelterwood cut when the seed trees are cut to provide wood and to remove competition from the new generation of trees. Removal generally takes place within two years after adequate regeneration has occurred, which is generally within one to seven years after initial logging.

Selection management: The application of logging and other actions needed to maintain continuous high-forest cover, recurring natural regeneration, and the orderly growth and development of trees through a range of diameter or age classes to provide a sustained yield of forest products. On large holdings, cutting is usually regulated by specifying the number or proportion of trees or particular sizes to retain within each area, thereby maintaining a planned distribution of size classes. Cutting methods that develop and maintain selection stands are individual-tree and group selection. Group selection is the removal of trees periodically in small groups resulting in openings that do not exceed one-tenth acre in size. A goal of selection is improvement of quality by continuously harvesting trees less likely to contribute to the long-range health of the stand.

All-species selection retains all species that are native to each site.

The Forest Service and some authors insist on the term "uneven-age management" in place of "selection management."

Caveat: On occasion, the Forest Service has resorted to narrower definitions in an effort to make selection appear non-adaptable to different sites and situations. Actually, one of the strengths of selection management is its flexibility.

Shelterwood cut: An even-aged silvicultural regeneration method under which a minority of the mature stand is retained as a seed source or protection during the regeneration period. The standing mature trees (usually ten to twenty per acre) are later removed in two or more cuttings.

Site Preparation: A general term for removing unwanted vegetation and slash from a site and exposing the soil before reforestation. May include ripping with a dozer scarifying tooth, burning, bulldozing ("shearing") and windrowing (pushing into long piles), chopping and rolling (pushing down and rolling over with heavy equipment): crushing (using huge equipment that chews up and ejects vegetation), injecting herbicides in live trees, spreading herbicides on the ground around live trees, or combinations of these.

Stand: A plant community with enough identity by location, topography, or dominant species to be considered as a unit. On federal lands, a stand is usually ten to one hundred acres.

Stringer: Two or more reserve trees not felled in a clearcut.

Understory: Plants growing beneath a canopy of other plants, particularly beneath the midstory, where there is one. Includes shrubs and groundcover (grasses, low forbs, ferns, mosses, fungi) in a forest.

Index

Books, Legislation, Organizations, Persons, Places
(except cities)
For additional lists, see Tables, 1, 2, and 3, and the catalogue
of selection managers, pages 113–114

A

Alabama, xii, 40, 42, 62, 108, 109, 110, 113
Alaska, xi, xviii, 20, 36, 56
alder, Red, 15
Alford, Jess, Jr., xi, 13, 15, 19
Allegheny NF, 8, 14, 87
Anderson, Nell, xii
Angelina NF, xx, xxi, 45, 74
Apalachicola NF, xvi, 88, 89, 112
Appalachian Mountains, xvi, 5, 8, 112
Arapaho NF, xviii
Aristida stricta (wiregrass), 15, 37, 88, 89
Arkansas, xii, 8, 42, 43, 48, 62, 81, 91, 93, 105
Arnold, Red, xii
ash: Green, xvii; Oregon, 15; White, xix, 41
aspen: Quaking, xvii, 100
azalea, Hoary, 41
Audubon Society, Seattle, 104

B

Babyfoot Lake, xviii
Baker, James B., 46, 81
  Wilson, xi
Baldcypress, xiii, xx

Ballentine, Audrey, 94
basswood, Carolina (linden), 92, 93, 97
bear: Black, 22, 48, 57, 88, 89; Grizzly, 39
Beason, David, xii
beech, American, xix, 92, 93
Beech drops, 93
beetle, Southern pine, 28, 31, 61, 62, 74, 75, 82
Bethel, Noel, 94
Big Thicket National Preserve, 56
Blackburn, W. H., 24
bloodroot, 88
bluestem, pinehills, 88
Bohn, Ira, xi
Boren, David, 95
Brothers, Robert, xi
Brush Disposal Act, 53, 54, 70
bunchberry, 18, 20
Bureau of Indian Affairs, 3, 4, 5, 70, 102, 104
Bureau of Land Management (BLM), 3, 4, 70, 71

C

California, xii, 4, 24, 25, 41, 46, 48, 57, 69
Campion, Tom, xi, 105